THE
LEADERSHIP
PLAYBOOK

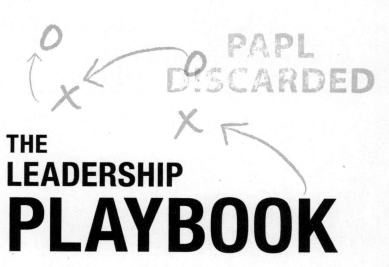

THE
LEADERSHIP
PLAYBOOK

Creating a Coaching Culture to Build Winning Business Teams

NATHAN JAMAIL

Gotham Books

GOTHAM BOOKS
Published by the Penguin Group
Penguin Group (USA) LLC
375 Hudson Street
New York, New York 10014

USA | Canada | UK | Ireland | Australia | New Zealand | India | South Africa | China
penguin.com
A Penguin Random House Company

LIBRARY OF CONGRESS CATALOGING-IN-PUBLICATION DATA
has been applied for.

ISBN 978-1-592-40866-5

Printed in the United States of America
10 9 8 7 6 5 4 3 2 1

Set in Adobe Garamond Pro
Designed by Spring Hoteling

To my son, Anthony, who can't believe that companies actually pay me for my advice; he has been getting my advice for the past eight years and can't pay me enough to *stop*.

And to my three princesses: Nyla, who is eleven going on thirty and is always taking care of her mom and little sisters, and Paige and Savannah, who don't really understand what Dad does, and when they are old enough to realize *still* probably won't understand what Dad does.

I talk about you all in every speech I give, because you are my everything. I love you very much.

CONTENTS

THE
LEADERSHIP
PLAYBOOK

FIRST PITCH

My son's Little League team lost its first game so bad that the umpires called the game under the "mercy rule." This rule, also known as the "slaughter rule," is invoked when one team has an insurmountable lead; it protects the emotional stability of the children, parents, and coach of the team getting skunked.

I was the coach.

The second game, we got a couple of runs but still lost. We won the third game. After our win, I got the kids together outside the dugout. With their parents looking on, I asked them if they felt better this week when we won than the previous weeks when we lost. They all said yes. "See, it does matter if you win or lose," I told them.

In sports, winning and losing matters. It matters. It doesn't matter if you are dealing with kids or colleagues: No team, period, can go onto a field expecting to lose the game. And it is a coach's job to instill this mind-set in the team—a mind-set that makes the team believe it can win every game and thus play every game to win. But as I told my Little League kids, "Winning is not just about results"; their desire to win as a team was much more important than the result of the game. After all, sometimes teams win just for showing up, and lose even though they do everything right. The important thing is to have a winning attitude—to lose with confidence and win with modesty.

Everything I said to my son's Little League team has the essential ingredients for success for any coach:

- Making the team members believe in themselves
- Mandating that the entire team work together
- Pushing the team to achieve success
- Encouraging a winning attitude
- Creating a team culture that supports all these things

Think about it: The people who helped make you successful in sports, school, or any part of your life that required your best performance were the ones who constantly challenged you, inspired you, drove you, and didn't take less than the best you could be—and they were *right* to do so. Our goal as business leaders should be to do the same with our people. But most times, we just don't.

That's because most businesses don't have coaching cultures and leaders who are coaches; they have management cultures and leaders who are managers. Coaches cannot thrive in management cultures that expect its leaders to pay attention to individuals more than to the team, handle problems reactively, focus on reforming the poorest performers, avoid conflict, and mostly just step back and let people do their jobs. A coaching culture expects the exact opposite of its leaders: to believe the team is more important than the results of an individual, get involved before action is needed, focus on the top performers who deserve their attention, embrace conflict, and always get on the field and practice with the team.

These are the missing elements in business and business leadership today: cultures that support a transformation of managers into coaches and help them develop the skills to do so. What if I told my Little League boys to work as a team and play with a winning attitude but didn't practice during the week or scrimmage game situations? We might never have won a game. It's not enough to talk about it. The same is true in business: We can't simply say we want our leaders to coach their teams; we need to show them how to be coaches. But for too long, the business world has lacked a clear and effective instruction on the skills, disciplines, and executable tasks necessary to turn leaders into coaches. That's no different from saying, "I want my accountant to be an engineer, but I'm not going to teach her how to become one." This is why the first parts of my book focus on understanding the differences between managing and coaching and then developing the fundamental skills—from practicing to making tough decisions to motivation—that leaders need to create and coach dynamic, motivated, high-functioning teams. Once I cover those skills, the last part of the book shows leaders what they need to do to change the culture of their department or business for supporting and sustaining their transformation from manager to coach.

Sounds great, right? So why aren't there more coaches and coaching cultures in business? Is it just the absence of a book like this? No. It's because coaching is hard. Coaching doesn't just happen. Coaching takes time and constant effort to make it the core of a business's leadership principles. Coaching does not work if it is optional. These lessons must be implemented and made mandatory. We can't simply try and fit coaching into our days. It never fits. Consider the first coaching activities we will cover in this book: practicing and scrimmaging. Professional business teams, unlike any professional sports teams, rarely practice. Why? It's not because we don't know that practice is essential to a team's success. But practicing takes time to set up and weeks and months of constant work to achieve great results. How can we possibly squeeze it into a list already overflowing with high-priority tasks? There's just no time! But everyone says that. We may be busy, but are we being productive?

Coaching makes us productive, but that productivity can be hard to wait for when we always feel we need some results now, now, NOW! That's another big obstacle to creating coaches and coaching cultures: There is little instant gratification in coaching. Gratification comes in achieving better results months down the road. When I show business leaders how to practice and scrimmage, they never leave the room saying, "Genius!" But while the overall results take time, the change in the team's morale just from paying attention to them and instilling a winning attitude happens much, much faster.

Truth is, there's a bigger reason we resist the changes needed to turn managers into coaches: We're afraid of what we might find. We're scared that when we begin to coach our people, we will find out that those people are not as good as we thought. That doesn't only make us scared, it makes us selfish. We don't want to deal with and take responsibility for all the inevitable work and conflict that comes from this change. Nobody likes making the tough decisions coaches need to make to move people up or out of the organization. Instead, we say things like "If I have to get rid of that guy, I will have to confront him directly and then do all his work while I work to replace him, and I don't want to do it." It's much easier to ignore the problem and hope it goes away. Yet it never does.

And I know this not because I write books about it, but because I have lived it myself. I learned all I know about coaching as an everyday businessperson, probably just like you. Before starting my own small businesses and becoming a consultant for dozens of large and small companies nationwide, I spent more than two decades leading teams in corporate America and was an executive sales director for a Fortune 500 company. I have seen the same leadership problems top to bottom in every one of them.

I'm the last person, however, who will say all this knowledge and experience makes me smarter than anyone else. I was a C- student, so I'm not always the sharpest tool in the shed. I can't pick out my own clothes, hairstyle, or furniture. Yet none of that has any effect on whether I—or anyone—can be a good coach. Coaches, in sports and business, often do not have (or never had) the skills of their best "players." Coaching has little to do with God-given talent, and past performance is no indicator of whether someone can be an effective leader, let alone a great coach. This is why it is the rare star athlete or smartest person in the room who becomes or even wants to become a coach.

To become a coach means challenging everything you think and do as a leader today. And that's what I want this book to do. I want to contradict the principles of management cultures you have been hearing and using

Coaching has to do with belief more than brilliance, and with attitude as much as aptitude.

for years and confront the things you have done in the past and believe to be right. What I don't want to do is make the words hard to follow. The fact is, I have a lot of half-read business books on my bookshelf written by people who have no idea what my "world" is like. I wanted to write a leadership book that people like me might actually finish and feel that—*finally*—there is a book that speaks "our" language.

To do this, I wrote the book similar to the way I speak from the stage, approaching concepts from different angles and with different purposes. I then repeat the core ideas for reinforcement so there is no need to memorize them as you read. In addition, you will not find a lot of international research or global theories in this book. I leave those to the wonks and scholars. Instead, I use real-life examples from my businesses and family, the companies I worked for, and the leaders and organizations I coach. As you probably guessed, I also use a lot of sports analogies, but I don't use them because I am an athlete or to make this a "man's book." I use sports analogies because I run my businesses like winning sports teams in which skill development and effective coaching makes the team better. The principles and activities are the same—female or male—and are described in simple X and O diagrams at the start of each chapter so you can see the "play" coming.

Before we get started with your leadership transformation, let me give you one last thought. Most of us have heard the phrase "work *on* your business instead of *in* your business," but I want to give you a coaching twist on it: **Work *on* your people, not *for* your people.** That's a big key to this book's working for you. I will show you the key coaching activities and cultural rules, but my sharing them will not be enough if you want to continue the transformation of individuals and overall culture to a winning, top-performing team. Regardless of their title, department, company, or industry, I believe leaders are paid to pay attention to, develop, and motivate their people and teams to perform better. Working with a diverse group of clients, not only in sales departments but also in engineering and operations, has taught me that the coaching principles I talked about in my first book, *The Sales Leaders Playbook*, are universally applicable and go much deeper than I imagined. Sure, companies can be successful and have functional cultures with leaders who are not coaches, but the best teams are those that are coached—not managed, *coached*—which is why this book starts with covering the differences between the two.

Enough of this already—let's play ball!

PART
ONE

Understand the Principles of Coaching

THE FIVE CRUCIAL DIFFERENCES BETWEEN MANAGING AND COACHING

Stop thinking like a manager and start thinking like a coach.

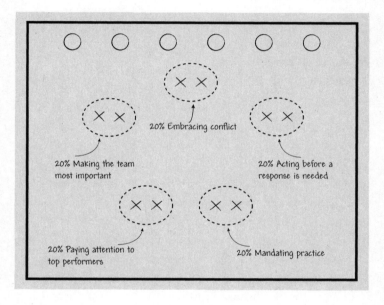

was talking to my dad, who is also a business partner of mine, about an employee at one of our dry cleaners. She had a bad attitude.

"What do you plan to do about her?" I asked.

"Nothing really," he said, "because we need her to run the store. She knows the business better than the others."

"So if she quit tomorrow, would we shut down the store?"

My dad chuckled and said, "Heck, no." He then mentioned that when she called, he cringed at seeing her number. He didn't like going to visit the store when she was there because it was such a "beatdown" (that's Texan for "misery").

"Dad, if you can't stand this person because she has a bad attitude, and you are the boss, imagine what her coworkers think or, even worse, our clients."

Most companies have leaders who are managers in management cultures.

Like too many business owners and leaders, my dad was avoiding dealing with this person for all the wrong reasons. He said he had talked to her about her attitude and had even written her up for it. What he *really* needed to do was deal with her once and for all, but he never took that final step because he still believed he needed her. I encouraged him to have one last meeting with her to make her immediately change her attitude or know we would immediately take the steps to terminate her. He finally did, and the employee decided she would be a better fit outside the organization. Did the store close as she left, taking all our dry cleaner experience with her? Of course not. The store stayed open, my father put in place a new manager with the right attitude, and business improved—both outside *and* inside. In fact, several employees and clients came to my father soon after and said, "Finally! What took you so long?"

In not dealing with this bad employee, my father, like so many business leaders, violated two of the five essential coaching principles that demonstrate two of the crucial differences between managing and coaching: No individual is more important than the team, and never avoid conflict. Then again, most businesses and their leaders, especially when things aren't going poorly, don't deal with problems like these or any others that may lurk below the surface. The expression "high water covers all rocks" comes to mind. But when things get rough—when the water recedes and the rocks appear—most leaders have little idea how to act effectively, pull their people together, and coach them as a team to perform better. They work in management cultures where leading means stepping back and letting people do their jobs, for better or worse. No need to rock the boat now. It will be high tide again soon, right? Maybe not.

This is a major reason I call the management-culture mentality fundamentally corrupt. Hire good people and let them do their jobs? That's a line handed down from outdated business books more than a generation old. Leaders today need to get involved and coach their teams to success, rather than manage them to mediocrity. Today's business isn't so much about today's economy as it is about today's leadership: Who is taking responsibility to actually *lead*? Technology and the competition move faster than ever before, and leaders need to implement a system for improvement and challenge their teams to compete at the speed of business today. Simply managing people and relying on them to develop themselves is not enough anymore. I'm not saying those management cultures were wrong for yesterday's business or that they can't work today; they just don't give leaders the best chance to succeed the way coaching cultures do. Yet most leaders don't understand what it means to coach, the differences between managing and coaching, or before all that, what it means to be a great leader.

> **Most companies NEED leaders who are coaches in coaching cultures.**

> **Great leaders aren't necessarily great coaches, but great coaches are great leaders.**

The Characteristics of Great Leaders

Great leaders are ethical, compassionate, and humble. They are great students and constantly strive to learn more. They are empathetic but not sympathetic, show resolve in the toughest times, and believe they can get something out of everybody, never dismissing anyone outright. Great leaders are strong and decisive without being arrogant. They never use fear to make the team fall in line, or use bravado to compensate for a fear of being vulnerable. Instead, they use vulnerability and humility to gain respect while still exuding confidence.

Great leaders always believe in themselves and their teams—that's how they get the teams' individual members to sacrifice for the good of those teams. The teams know these leaders make them better and thus strive to please them. As a result, great leaders have a loyal—even blind—followership. In short, their teams love and trust them and their vision. But the ability to create a vision alone does not make a great leader—the ability to have it, communicate it, and get people to act on it does. When companies want people to communicate their visions or missions, they put them on cards, coffee mugs, posters, and newsletters. Great leaders know that stuff goes only so far. They know they must get their teams to do more than read those words. They must get them to believe in those words and make them part of the team's everyday vocabulary without ever thinking about it.

> **Coaching doesn't change who we are as leaders; it changes what we do.**

Great Leaders versus Great Coaches

The differences between great leaders and great leaders who are coaches lie in their activities and actions. Leaders who don't do the proactive activities and actions of coaching covered in Part Two of this book are not coaches. Leaders who choose to sit back and develop their people through reactive management activities designed to maintain the status quo are not coaching. They may have the potential to be a coach but not if they continue to sit back, refuse to get more deeply and proactively involved with their people, and say things like "My employees don't want me telling them how to do their job, and I don't want to do that!" Unfortunately, this line is just one of the excuses leaders make for not taking the time to coach.

For the record, leaders who are coaches are more engaged with their teams, but they are not always in their employees' faces, getting in the way for the sake of getting involved and micromanaging everything all the time (although micromanaging is a coaching tool and can be approached positively, as we will see later on). Coaches just don't fear involvement as they make sure employees doing *their* "thing" are aligned with the *team's* "thing." Yet understanding this and saying you're ready to learn and implement the skills necessary to coach won't mean much if you don't understand the differences between managing and coaching. Turning managers into coaches begins not with action and activities but with accepting the fundamental differences between managing and coaching.

The Five Crucial Ways Managing Differs from Coaching

1. **Belief in the team:** Coaches believe in a team culture and the need to be connected to that team constantly so everyone performs better. Managers focus on individuals and then disconnect to let them "just do their jobs."

2. **Conflict management:** Coaches make use of conflict to move team members up in the organization or out. Managers try to avoid conflict.
3. **Involvement:** Coaches get involved before action is needed (to prevent problems from developing). Managers react and get involved only when they are needed (when there is a problem and often too late).
4. **Employee focus:** Coaches focus on top performers (those who deserve attention). Managers focus on poor performers (those who need attention).
5. **Team building:** Coaches are always practicing and scrimmaging to make their teams better. Managers rarely practice.

Now let's translate these differences into the five essential principles of coaching every coach must follow.

The Five Essential Principles of Coaching

1. Make the team more important than any individual.
2. Don't avoid conflict—use it!
3. Act before a response is needed.
4. Pay attention to top performers and focus on making more of them.
5. Mandate EVERYBODY to practice.

Every one of these principles informs the coaching activity chapters in Part Two of this book. Skill practice, making tough decisions, rewards and recognitions, building your bench, game plans, setting goals, peer presentations . . . all of them require coaches to appreciate the importance of these principles. So let's take the time to discuss them in a little more depth, especially the first one, which will be the biggest shock for most leaders who are managers.

Coaching Principle #1
Make the team more important than any individual

Think about those star athletes who were or are great players but have bad attitudes that alienate their teammates, coaches, owners, and fans. Their talent may be undeniable, but so is their unlikability. They put themselves above everyone, and despite putting up some big numbers and occasionally playing in championship games, they rarely lead their teams to the ultimate victory. Most of these players, despite their God-given talent and gaudy stats, eventually destroy the team's chemistry, and unless bound by a long-term contract their teams now regret, those teams release them, again and again. Sure, they usually sign somewhere else. Other teams and coaches try to work with them, thinking the results they generate may offset any personal problems. Maybe these players mature. Maybe they find the coaches who can turn them around. But usually those players aren't about contributing to the success of anyone but himself or herself and are eventually let go again.

In business, we have the same superstars with good results and bad attitudes. Problem is, we don't usually fire people like that or even confront them; we leave them alone. Even when their results decline a bit. Even when the team can't stand them.

Even when *we* can't stand them. We isolate them so they can "do their job" and not annoy the team. We effectively say to them, "Hey, you don't play very well with others, but you make me money, so I'm going to let you do your thing, keep you away from the team, and not push you to do anything outside your comfort zone. Carry on!" A lot of times, we actually try to give these people *more* responsibility as a "reward." That's like rewarding an irresponsible child: My kid keeps slacking on his responsibilities, so I'm going to teach him how to be responsible by letting him babysit his little sister. Not a good plan.

These employees, like those problem star athletes, need to be coached up or coached out for the good of the team *regardless of their individual results*. I'm not saying those results are not important. I'm saying the exact opposite. Results are so important that to think that one person with a bad attitude is the only one who can achieve those results, that those results cannot be better, and that those results are contributed in a completely positive manner is a mistake.

Ask yourself this question: Is this person with the bad attitude really generating the results that he or she could be generating or are you accepting them so you don't have to deal with him or her? Leaders may think they are helping people with bad attitudes by being "nice" and not firing them. But we're actually being self-serving; we have authority to act but don't want to take the risk of losing the revenue stream or the perceived success. We're also being cruel to everyone else on the team by making them suffer for the results of one individual. Heck, *we* don't like them; imagine what everyone else thinks.

How much have we actually looked into the results of those good performers with the bad attitudes? We assume that because people generate productive results, it is because of something only they can do. Thus, we assume they are valuable. But we usually don't know for sure. We see 10 percent growth and think, *Great!* but never consider that replacing the person might generate even more growth. Often, it turns out, they are productive in spite of themselves. Maybe it is the territory they cover, the demand for the product or service they work on, the kind of projects they get assigned, a particular whale of a client, or a responsibility that is so great that they take credit for it because they have the closest connection. And are we even considering how this person affects the team? Are they causing other people on the team to perform less? It is not just about results but the energy that you and the team feel from them.

> **It is the results that matter—the results of the team.**

Knowing this, why do leaders keep people with bad attitudes simply because of the results? Laziness is a big factor; it takes work to deal with these people. But a big part of it is fear of the conflict that comes from making these tough decisions (as we will see in the next principle in this chapter). It is also fear of what will happen when these people leave: How will I replace those results? (The answer is in Chapter 6: "Build Your Bench.") What if I make a mistake and they are as good as I think? But they never are.

We'll cover this in more depth later, but for now know—and I have not found anyone to dispute me on this—I have never seen a person with a bad attitude and good results leave a company and the overall results suffer long-term. In fact, when a company loses that person, the overall results, productivity, and effectiveness of the team usually *increase* long-term. I always tell prospective clients that I believe one of the greatest mistakes a business can make is to base a short-term decision on a long-term need or desire. In most cases, the fear of the loss is much greater than the actual loss.

I had this happen with a Fortune 100 technology client whose vice president of engineers was not nice and was always negative. He questioned and bucked every change his bosses asked him to implement. When asked to do peer reviews, he refused. When they brought me in to talk to him about coaching, he said, "My employees don't need coaching. They are engineers and just need to do their jobs." As the VP resisted coaching again and again, I told my client that he should begin looking for the man's replacement. He agreed but was too afraid to take action. "Nathan, you don't understand," he said. "He's respected in the community and the industry. He actually writes laws for our industry. He testifies to local governments on what should and should not be a regulation in our industry. He's invaluable."

But he wasn't invaluable. He was just someone with a bad attitude. He was the only one tooting his horn. I asked my client if they had actually seen him write those laws or had spoken to the people he testified for. Was he making his contributions bigger than they actually were to protect himself from being more closely examined and his bosses from discovering he was just smoke and mirrors? After all, his peers didn't like him, his bosses didn't like him, and I was sure that if my client took the time to actually speak to the people he said he did all this work for, they would say they didn't like him much either. That's what eventually happened when my client dug deeper. He finally faced his vice president and moved him out of that position and eventually out of the company, with no regrets. He tells me, "Ever since that person left, the team has been so much better and everyone has stepped up." That's because he was stifling everyone else and bringing them down.

Now, before you start to say, "I agree, Nathan, but attitude is subjective, and HR won't let me deal with people for things like that unless those bad attitudes create a hostile workplace," let me say that this is not true. Let's dispel that myth right now: We *can* legally fire someone for having a bad attitude because *a bad attitude is bad performance*. Employees don't need to be racist, sexist, or any other "ist" and create hostile work environments for leaders to act. We just need to be clear about what the bad attitude is, communicate it to the employee, and document it with verbal and written warnings. I fired dozens of people with good results but bad attitudes when I was in corporate America, and I rarely had an HR issue, because I made sure the employees knew they needed to step up or step out, and I documented everything.

HR doesn't want a company's leaders to keep bad people; they just want those leaders to be better prepared when we deal with those people. In fact, most companies have written processes for dealing with bad attitudes. (If yours doesn't, a simple Google search for "firing an employee with a bad attitude" will generate hundreds of reliable results from a variety of industries and experts.) Still, we love using HR and legal as an excuse for why we cannot hold everyone accountable for their attitudes, so we just don't do it. That is why so many employees may not even know they *have* a bad attitude. This is a problem with leadership, not the employee. Because the manager has never told them they have a bad attitude nor documented it, they don't want to start dealing with it now. It's not worth the fight.

I will admit that documenting bad attitudes can be hard to do—you can feel it but struggle to put it into words. It is easier when that person is a "Life-Sucker" or any of the most common types that we will discuss in more detail in Chapter 7, but the best place to start is to write it down every time someone does something or says something that makes you cringe or just feel disappointed. And ask these questions about every person on your team:

- When you are around them, do they make you feel good, bad, or indifferent?
- Do they want to commit to the team or do they just seem content to have a job?
- Do they want to improve and make the team better or are they comfortable with the status quo?

I believe anyone who doesn't make us feel good, want to be a part of the team, and improve to make that team and our companies better has a bad attitude. That's right, it's not just the jerks and negative people like the one at my technology client who clearly have bad attitudes. It can be a person spinning his wheels, with no hunger to do better, complacent about generating okay results, and sending a signal to the team that this is okay if they do it too. Coaches must sit down with people like this and ask if they really want to be with the company. These are required conversations.

So it's not just the worst attitudes and poorest performers who affect the team and a coach's ability to lead that team. It can be the employee who has been with you for ten years, is nice enough, knows your business and industry, contributes a small amount to the bottom line but doesn't contribute a whole lot to the team, and just wants to be left alone to do his or her job. Most of us see that person as loyal. Why upset someone who isn't losing you money and has been with you a long time? Sorry, that person is *tenured,* not loyal, and isn't a team player. That's a key management misperception. Stop paying them and see how loyal they are. Loyalty cannot be based on time served. Loyalty must be based on growth and contribution to the team. If an employee has been with you for ten years, contributes to the success of the team, *and* still gives you everything he or she has got, then that employee is loyal. Anyone else is just collecting paychecks.

Yes, everyone contributes in their own way in all departments and divisions and across any team. Every team has players with different responsibilities. Therefore, I do believe that, in coaching, we must

> **Complacency can be just as dangerous to the team's morale as negativity.**

treat people differently, because everyone has different strengths and weaknesses. What I'm talking about here is when leaders do something coaches never do in sports: Accept team members who, regardless of title or responsibility, are clearly not or are no longer the best people for their jobs. To define team contribution, answer the following questions about everyone who works for you, notwithstanding their tenure:

- Do the people in each position deliver the absolute best results they can and thus make the team better as a result?
- At every level of the company or team, do your people perform at the top of their game or are they making excuses for why they aren't?
- Are the people you have the best people or are you accepting results because of how long someone has been doing a job?
- Are your people adapting to new technologies and ways of doing business or doing it the way they used to because "that's the way we've always done it"?
- Do other team members have to do more for what one person is not doing?

In sports, when players wind up on the wrong side of the answers to these questions, they retire or they get cut. They may give it their all, but sometimes that is just not enough. It doesn't mean they need to leave the sport, but they do need to leave the field. They might become backups or utility players on their or another team for a few years, but if they can't compete at the highest level, they get backup pay.

In corporate America, that shocks us. Backup pay for my most senior people? No, your top-performing people should be getting top-performing pay regardless of their age or experience. I'm talking about people who may not belong in their positions anymore and at the salaries they are used to because they are not contributing to the team the way they should. It doesn't have to be someone who has been there a long time. A job that requires travel or long hours may have suited someone who was young and single when you hired them but now, a few years later, they are married with kids and the pressure and responsibilities are too much. Perhaps there are roles in which people can deliver the results you expect, whether it is research and development or policy writing or something else that works for the team, but not in the position they were originally. They can contribute more to the team in that new role. They just can't expect to get paid the same way.

That's how coaches put their teams over any individual. If someone is not fully contributing to the team—no matter how experienced they are—tell them. You can say, "Listen, you are one of my top guys. You've been here a long time. But I need you to help me achieve our goals and help the team focus on practice, commitment, and teamwork or else we need to find a better fit for you outside the organization." Leaders can confront the situation and coach that person out of it or coach him out of the company. It might just be for the better of the employee too. Sports teams and businesses are filled with stories of skilled people who let a bad or wrong attitude get the best of them but then thrived with a change of scenery.

Problem is, all of this is easier said than done, and chances are that this person you confront is going to disagree with you. That's why coaches learn to embrace conflict.

Coaching Principle #2
Don't avoid conflict—use it!

Most leaders I meet say they understand the importance of having good attitudes on their team. I tell them I believe that a good team attitude is mandatory, not important, and they agree. Then I ask them if they have that person we just described on their team, someone who makes them decent money but has a bad attitude. Almost all of them do. So I tell them, "Then tomorrow confront that person and fire him or her."

"Whoa, I'm not willing to go that far!" they say.

Why not confront these people? It's not because we don't know that person is a problem. It's not because we think firing is the only solution; this might turn around, once we confront them. It's because many leaders avoid this and any conflict. The best coaches I ever had never shied away from conflict, especially when it came to my performance and attitude. Without being abusive, they got that finger in my face and challenged me to do better. They told me when I made mistakes. They held me accountable and didn't let me get away with anything. And they made me better because of it.

I'm not saying conflict is ever easy, but look on the bright side: Leaders at least know that none of this should come as a surprise to the person with the problem or bad attitude, if only because they have documented everything, as outlined in the final coaching principle. In truth, right there, the conflict has begun. They have asked for the commitment to the team. They might discover that there are temporary personal issues causing the problems or that there has been an irreversible decline in skills. Whatever it is, start and continue to have the difficult conversations. Speak respectfully, clearly, and most important, di-

> **It's easy to be a bad parent, a bad coach, or a bad leader.**

rectly, but be willing to get in a poor performer's face and say, "Hey, that sucks and it needs to change" or "Listen, we have tried to make this work and I am sorry, but it just has not worked. . . ."

For example, Jim has been in the sales department at one of my major technology clients for seven years. For the first five years, his numbers placed him in the top 15 percent. But last year, he dropped down to the middle, and this year, he continued to drop. Jim is nice and doesn't really make waves, but his results are clearly down and his drive seems gone. I say "seems"

> **It's hard to make up for it.**

because that's all my client knows for sure. Jim may be a thorn in his manager's spreadsheet, but his manager ignored Jim when he was a top performer and now waited until Jim was really in decline to even contemplate confronting him. That leaves my client three options for dealing with Jim, in order of least to most difficult:

1. Keep ignoring him (and hope he'll recover his mojo or just go away).
2. Fire him.
3. Coach him back to the top.

Most leaders who have been minted in management cultures choose option one in dealing with Jim: the path of least resistance. When things get really bad, they might turn to option two. But note how coaching is even harder than firing someone.

Coaching takes more time and conflict beyond the disciplinary and termination conversations. Holding people accountable takes time. Being the person who's challenging others to do better all the time takes time.

In this case, assuming Jim could still be a top performer, my client chose to coach him. She asked him to recommit his energy to the team. She firmly, but respectfully and calmly, pointed out that Jim's performance in the last two years had really declined. She asked him the right questions to see if he was aware of the problem and capable of committing to the team. She listened to his response but was careful to note if he accepted responsibility or simply blamed anyone or anything he could, using the meeting as a platform for complaining about her, the company, the industry, the world, his mother. . . . In the end, she told Jim her goal was to get his performance back to where it was, and it needed to be there or well on its way in sixty days. If after sixty days he was not able to get there, she would help Jim find a better fit in or outside the company, where everyone could be happier. My client wanted to believe Jim could reach the top again, so the offer was genuine, and she offered him the attention and access to her that she now gave to other top performers (see Coaching Principle #4). No matter what, though, Jim's performance could now be accurately gauged to see if he could keep his eye on the goal, improve his skills, and strive to commit to be part of a top-performing team.

Did it work? No. Jim realized he was no longer a great fit for the team and found another job, and my client, who was working hard on transitioning from manager to coach, quickly worked to find the right replacement. With Jim, as with a talented professional athlete who is stuck in a rut after years with the same team, all the attention now may not make him any happier or reverse the problem. Maybe it had nothing to do with my client in the first place; Jim had some personal problems that were putting him in a rut, and there was nothing she could do about it. A change of teams and coaches might be just what Jim, like that athlete, needed to shake things off and see a career resurgence.

You don't have to be in sales to recognize a "Jim" in your department or business. You don't need numbers and spreadsheets to measure a bad attitude or declining skills. But if you can't take the necessary steps and see the power of conflict through coaching, your Jim will never change.

Coaching Principle #3
Act before a response is needed

Dealing with bad performance or attitudes and embracing conflict can be a real culture shock for managers learning to become coaches. But that's the consequence of leading in the way we have been leading: We don't approach problems head-on. We hope they'll go away, making excuse after excuse for not handling them. Yet they never go away. The good news is that coaching activities like scrimmaging, quarterly game plans that actually get implemented, and peer presentations, which we cover in Part Two of this playbook, all help leaders to recognize and deal with problems before they become bigger problems or even problems at all.

At Sprint, I took the idea of a quarterly game plan even further: I held mandatory quarterly full-day training sessions for my team of managers who ran sales teams across Southern California. This wasn't just Nathan University. The meetings were designed as massive interactive learning experiences covering a variety of topics to help us better understand the business behind our activities and to perform better as a team. The topics weren't just sales based either. The managers worked in small groups and covered everything from learning the roles of finance and human resources to showing how to read a P&L statement (so the team could understand how profit and loss are actually calculated for the business the next time they wanted to take a client to lunch or run a special promotion). We did presentation skill breakouts and practiced day-to-day situations like overcoming objections and greeting customers. Every quarter, we would decide which topics to change and which to keep, depending on what was most important to the business and needed the most improvement.

**Managers react.
Coaches get involved.**

What made these meetings great was the level of involvement they required from my entire team and me. The meetings were my way to get my team connected and learning regularly. They forced us to improve on a more frequent schedule than the usual annual meeting cycle of most companies. We would effectively kick-start the next quarter, make it better by taking what we struggled with the previous quarter and working on it together. The learning went beyond quarterly too: My managers would take what they learned and use it in their weekly meetings with their teams.

At first, my boss was dubious. "Jamail," he said, "how can you afford to take your people out of the market for eight hours every quarter?" I told him, "I'd rather have a motivated and connected team for eighty-nine days of a ninety-day quarter than an unmotivated and disconnected team for ninety days. I want to put you and me in a position to be successful by preparing them to be successful."

I also could afford to do it because the cost was immaterial to the reward. My boss initially looked at these meetings in terms of straight dollar costs—the fact that my managerial team was out of the field for four days a year plus travel, hotel, and a cheap space to hold the event. (I used the meeting rooms at a bowling alley in exchange for five hundred dollars' worth of bowling and food afterward.) But I saw the cost benefit in terms of eliminating many more unproductive field days and bad interactions because of the work being done at these meetings. Every quarter, my managers were refreshed, focused, and motivated, and I had a better sense of how each of them was doing and where future problems might lie. All this led to significant benefits: We went from being the worst market in the country to the number one market in eighteen months.

What's that? You love this concept, but you don't have time to get so involved? You're too busy dealing with all these problems and putting out the fires your people set and you still need to accomplish your own goals? Well, if you regularly coach your people on how to stop setting fires, you won't have as many fires to put out, and that means more time for everything on your list.

And don't think for a moment that just because you don't lead sales teams as I did, actions and activities like these meetings won't work for your department or industry. Can you really look in the mirror and say that because you're a leader of a creative or engineering team, there is nothing your team can work on together to make them better? Leaders of any kind of team benefit from regular interactions that help push the team forward and address what is to come rather than simply rehashing what has been.

Going through a person's performance postmortem is like an autopsy: That body is dead.

Rehashing what has been is only feedback, which we ask for and give constantly as leaders, from the smallest tasks (how we thought a meeting went) to the largest events (performance reviews). This is why leaders typically consider feedback coaching. But feedback is only *part* of coaching, and it will not help coaches act *before* a response is needed. That's because all feedback is reactive and focuses on the past. This does not mean feedback is unimportant. Offering feedback regularly is our chance as leaders to tell our employees one-on-one all the good things they did and to offer a few helpful points to ponder and suggestions for improvement. Leaders usually feel pretty good about those meetings, but it is no substitute for the larger activities of coaching.

Feedback can also *create* problems if it is done only when things go wrong and any positive feedback becomes just a crap sandwich before the beatdown starts. I have leaders at all the organizations I work with tell me they get involved only when their teams have a problem or can't do something. That means every time that leader gets involved, it is a negative. When the team sees the leader coming, they think, "Uh-oh. What did we do wrong?" *We can't coach someone who views our involvement as a negative reaction.* When a leader's involvement is a consequence of an employee not doing well, the leader, not the employee, has violated this principle of coaching.

The activities of coaching that support these principles, such as the quarterly meetings, need to happen in addition to and *before* feedback, *before* performance reviews on presentations and events, *before* someone picks up the phone and destroys even one business relationship, *before problems happen.* If this sounds like controlling or micromanaging, that is not the intention—rather, it is a positive way to bestow attention on the team and make everyone better by getting involved (see Chapter 11). And our best people deserve that extra attention.

Coaching Principle #4
Pay attention to top performers
and focus on making more of them

When an NFL team has the number one draft pick, the team doesn't just hand the kid a jersey and say, "See you on Sunday." The coach's job is to take that top talent and mold him into something better. This is equally true with top-performing veterans in sports who are looking for a fresh start. Take Peyton Manning. He was already one of the greatest quarterbacks in the NFL, but when he joined the Denver Broncos, his coach's job was to push him to be better, and Manning's job was to commit to the team and give them his all. They nearly made it to the Super Bowl his first season there.

If Peyton Manning were an employee in almost any business, his manager would have hired him for big money and then . . . just left him alone. They would probably train him on the basics of the new team and its systems, and then throw him on the field to "do his thing." How is that fair to the person who is bringing you all this greatness? If you are the top guy putting in fifty to sixty hours a week and you're getting left alone, you're getting robbed. You bring all this energy and passion to the job and what you get in return is to be left alone and ignored? How is anyone helping you get from where you are to where you want to go? How can a leader expect you to help the team get to where it needs to go?

This is a major reason leaders struggle in business: They do everything the opposite of what coaches do to make their teams great. In this case, they don't focus on the top. I know this notion flies in the face of conventional wisdom, but it reinforces why I think the dumbest piece of business advice is "Hire great people and let them do their job." That's the reason businesses leave their top players alone. In fact, it is seen as an achievement in many companies that people get so good at what they do that their bosses leave them alone.

Coaches in business should focus their energy more on the top just as coaches in sports focus most on the first string. The second- and third-string players always know they can become part of the first string if they commit to the team, work hard, strive to do more to earn their opportunities, and catch the coach's attention by delivering bigger results. A coach's biggest problem is not when the third-string players, who are busting their tails, complain about not getting enough time. The problem is when the third-string players don't even care.

Everyone who hears me say this responds that it makes sense to them. They leave my presentations pumped and ready. But at eight o'clock Monday morning, it's back to putting out fires and trying to fix the problems of the weakest em-

> **Managers spend too much time with the people who need the attention instead of those who deserve the attention.**

ployees while letting the top people handle everything themselves. These leaders tell me again and again, "If I could get rid of my problems first, I could spend time with my people. But I can't get rid of my problems, so I can't spend time with my people. So, therefore, they're not getting better. . . ." This is all a self-fulfilling prophecy. My advice is let the buildings burn, man. Sometimes we have to sacrifice. At Pearl Harbor, the triage nurses famously marked patients with lipstick with an *F* for "fatally wounded," meaning there was nothing the doctors could do; the patient will die no matter what. In business, we tend to do the opposite—try to fix what can't be saved and ignore the top performers.

When people tell me this sounds like I play favorites and

spend all my time with such-and-such top people, I don't deny it. I admit it creates some conflict in the ranks, which I embrace, as you know. But I am honest about what I am doing. I tell the team that I spend time with the people who are top performers, have great attitudes, and make me a lot of money. I also let them know that if they commit to the team, I'll commit to them in the same way. I always gave my new and best people attention early and fast. They deserved that attention beyond training because I decided to bring them onto the team. I gave them access to my calendar and expected them to book it. I gave them everything I've got, to see if they could get to the first string, or I would get them out. Hire fast, fire faster, I always say.

My goal was to make my involvement a reward for doing well rather than a consequence of doing something wrong. But I also knew my top performers would get on my calendar only if they perceived me as someone who could help them do better. If they perceived me as someone who's just going to judge them and bring them down, not add value or help make the deals, work, or skills better, they would not want to be involved with me. A Fortune 100 financial company I work with struggled with this situation when their leadership team wanted their corporate liaisons to go on appointments with their agents and help generate better deals. None of the agents asked them to go. Now, if you were an agent and you knew taking me, your liaison, on a call with you would lead to your closing more deals and making more money, how many calls would you want me to go on? All of them. Then, unless the agents are so insecure that they can't have anyone else around when they go on appointments, the reason they don't want me around is that they don't think I'm good enough to take.

I can't tell you who your top performers are, or what the specific criteria should be to measure your people, but I can tell you that every company, large or small, and every department in any business in any industry has at least a top and a bottom. Leaders need to identify them so they can decide how to approach the activities for those team members. If the leader is like me, in a sales leadership position or a numbers-based department, you might think this kind of ranking is easier: Just look at the numbers. But the biggest mistake we can make as leaders of these teams is to use "the scoreboard" as the sole criterion for ranking employees. Great sports coaches don't say, "Well, we won twenty-one to nothing and we're six-and-oh, so it doesn't matter that my quarterback has thrown one touchdown and twenty interceptions; he's the most important position, so he's my number one player." That quarterback's coach is not only going to focus on what the quarterback didn't do in practice activities but also start looking for someone who might move up or into that position.

Think you don't have a bottom—that all your people are good? Ask yourself, as the team leader, if your boss or your most important client said you were the same as everyone on your team, would you feel complimented, insulted, or ripped off? Almost everyone I have worked with says they would feel insulted or ripped off. They believe, right or wrong, they are better than some of their peers. Don't you think your employees think the same thing? So how do you know where your employees rank if you don't have any numbers to put on the scoreboard?

- Ask your best clients or customers.
- Ask other employees at the company.
- Ask yourself, who's the person you go to when you need to get something done?
- Ask yourself, if you've got X number of team members and can take only one of them with

you to a new job or to start a new company, who would it be? If you could take only two, who would they be? Three?

• Knowing what you know today, who would you not hire tomorrow?

Answering these questions will give leaders their top, middle, and bottom and a clear path to ranking the whole team. Coaches then know who is on the first string and who is on the third string—who the starters are and who the role players are—and can get them all ready to coach accordingly. That's why a ranking is only the first part of the coaching equation and why the coaching principles, skills, and culture are so important. The principles keep us grounded, the culture provides the time to create coaching activities, and the time allows coaches to pursue those activities as a team.

In the end, for many new coaches in business, the hardest part of obeying the ranking principle is learning what to do with the middle. During breaks in workshops, leaders regularly come up to me and say, "I love how you talk about the top and the bottom, but my top performers are fine. I'm more concerned about the middle. I have to move the people in the middle."

I tell them, "Don't focus so much on the middle. Make them want to be top performers. To move the middle, focus on the top performers, remove the bottom, and make the middle desire to be part of the top because that's where the attention and action are!"

Does this mean fire the lowest-paid employees and pay attention to the highest-paid ones? No. There are top, middle, and bottom people in any department and division, from customer service to marketing to engineering to accounting. Leaders throughout a company should think of their middle people as metal and their top and bottom people as magnets. Make sure the top has the most magnets and that's where the middle will gravitate.

Say a leader has ten employees—two in the top, six in the middle, and two in the bottom. Conventional wisdom tells that leader to leave the top two people alone and work with the middle as if they are the top. That middle is comfortable, approachable, and seemingly fixable. It is also the straightest path to mediocre performance for the team. It is easy and safe to manage to the middle.

Sure, you need more top performers—but not at the expense of your current top performers. If being in the top means getting no attention, those top performers will either look to go somewhere else or, maybe even worse, refuse to work as hard. Now, if the top performers don't care, and the middle is so comfortable, why would anyone leave the middle? Why would anyone in the middle want to move up? They can work less hard and get all the attention they need—even if they fall off a bit, no one ever gets fired anyhow. Push the top to grow. And don't just ignore the bottom. Remove it and watch the middle want to move in the right direction.

> **The way to move the middle up is to chop off the bottom and grow the top.**

This is why I say the 80-20 rule is a terrible thing to abide by in coaching. The 80-20 rule, or the Pareto principle, dates back to 1897 and the Italian economist Vilfredo Pareto, who found that 80 percent of most nations' wealth was controlled by just 20 percent of the population. Other economists soon started noticing the same unequal patterns elsewhere; just a few causes accounted for most effects. Today, the 80-20 rule has become shorthand for saying 20 percent of whatever you are measuring is responsible for 80 percent of your results, such as 20 percent of your customers are responsible for 80 percent of your profits. The idea is that a few things are disproportionately responsible for most results or effects.

To me, the Pareto principle is not a rule; it is a result and another self-fulfilling prophecy caused by inaction by managers in management cultures. If the top 20 percent of a football team produces 80 percent of the results, that team will never be the best. They will be, at most, good and very likely average. The same is even truer in business: The top 20 percent of the team cannot produce 80 percent of the results and have the manager simply leave them alone. Our top-performing people need to know that they must keep performing and improving their skills to keep their jobs and that we are watching and giving them the tools. The top performers should be the first ones on the practice field working with the coaches and inspiring the new hires, the middle, and even the other top performers to take them on. Otherwise, the top 20 percent is never going to grow any bigger, and the middle will have no reason to aspire to be in the top.

Coaching Principle #5
Mandate EVERYBODY to practice

I have never heard anyone say, "Let's manage this team to the top!" Leaders do not *manage* to grow. They manage to *maintain*. When you are managing, you're not interested in developing the team and making everyone stronger; you're interested in managing the business so you can make more money and increase profits.

In sports, teams achieve these peak levels by practicing. A coach says, "We are going to practice all week, every week, before the game." Professional athletes practice 90 percent of their time.

But in business, teams do not practice at all. How and what to practice is what we will cover in Chapter 1. What I want you to understand now is why we don't practice: Our leaders do not demand it from us because they don't see it as important or valuable. Sure, we train new hires and then maybe once a year we do some kind of team "training" or new product development, or we retrain people on existing office protocols or using new systems. Don't confuse this training with coaching. Trainings are like "new year, new you" approaches to exercise and dieting: They happen and then they are gone.

In business, a coach must say all the time, "We've got a big job ahead of us, and to do it, we are all going to prepare and hone our skills." I call this kind of practice "scrimmaging." Scrimmaging is about preparing to play the game. Scrimmaging is about trying something out, improving skills, discovering new possibilities. If the team stinks when scrimmaging, that's fine. Better to find out before "game time" what skills need improvement and which players need more help. The team learns how to work better together.

So how, exactly, do we find the time to do this scrimmaging while we are on the job and *doing* our job? After all, offices are not practice fields. Practice is what an athlete is paid for to get ready for the games, but work isn't practice; work is always "game day." But it's not. Here's the real truth: Most people think they get paid to do whatever task they are doing. This is just a convenient excuse for not finding the time for something new, such as coaching.

Of course, we can't practice 90 percent of the time as they do in sports, but are you really saying that your work would not benefit from practicing something you need to do just 5 percent of the time? Five percent of a forty-hour workweek means finding two hours a week to take an essential step toward being a coach. And yes, I do believe we get paid to practice as leaders in business because practice is crucial to personal and team development. I don't care what your title or industry is. I don't care if you are a leader in human resources, sales, finance, nursing, social work, design, engineering, or any other area you can think of: Leaders get paid to develop their people, and if they are not doing it, then they may not understand their job description.

Never mind that almost everyone I know believes that when you practice something, you get better at it—maybe not perfect but absolutely better. In fact, when we hear about athletes skipping or slacking off in practice, we say they don't care and we get angry with them. We call them arrogant. I don't know if I would say we are being arrogant as business leaders when we don't practice, but when it comes to our businesses, saying we don't have time for it confuses having knowledge of what to do with having the best skills, the most confidence, and becoming better at what we do. **Knowledge in and of itself isn't power; it is what we do with knowledge that makes it powerful.**

Coaches never think they know it all, and don't expect their teams to know it all either.

The sales reps at one of the largest building products manufacturing companies in North America used to get fewer than 5 percent of their referrals from trade shows, and the divisional president at the time wanted to know why. So he flew all the reps into town for a national trade show a night early to change things up. He flew me in and we met with the reps at the hotel and told them we were going to practice what to say when someone walks into the booth at the show the next day.

"That's stupid; we know how to do this," they all said before condescendingly agreeing to the task.

Not surprisingly, their performance was awful. They were

stammering, using canned lines, and giving wrong information. When we pointed that out to them, they said, "This isn't real." Of course it isn't. But usually the only time I hear "it's not real" is as an excuse for poor performance. If they can't do it in practice and don't have the right approach, rapport, and information, how can they do it right when it counts? The divisional president sat them down and walked them through the right way to approach a potential customer and to provide the correct information. From there, the reps started to prepare and practice with real purpose.

Coaches know they need to make their teams scrimmage as if everything is real and to practice like we play so that when we get the real chance to play, we maximize every opportunity we can. As for the building products manufacturing company, the reps got the message and for two hours they practiced and got pretty good. The next day at the trade show, they got more leads and more referrals than they ever had. Today, they practice the night before trade shows and the weeks leading up to them, and now get the lion's share of their referrals at the events.

What this company learned is that, without practicing, you do business as usual—not better. When employees do their jobs but don't practice, they also do those jobs on the safe side. They don't take chances. They don't push themselves. Great coaches in business know practicing helps teams learn and improve quickly. That's why mandating practice for everyone is both an essential coaching principle and the first activity in becoming a coach.

PART
TWO

Be a Coach

Chapter 1
MANDATE SKILL PRACTICE
AND PLAYER DEVELOPMENT

Business skills need development and improvement just as much as athletic skills do.

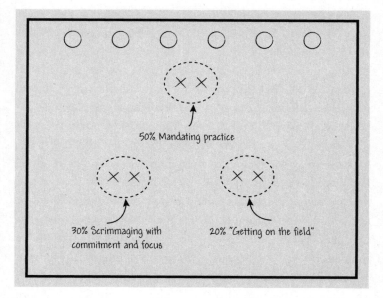

50% Mandating practice

30% Scrimmaging with commitment and focus

20% "Getting on the field"

How many times have you walked up to the front desk of a hotel or restaurant, made eye contact with an employee, and said, "How are you today?" and he or she replies, "Welcome to Such-and-Such Place"?

Huh? How about you answer the question I asked? Unfortunately, I can't say this surprises me when it happens. I was giving a presentation to a client in the hospitality industry and asked the audience, "How many people actually practice with your people on how to say hello? I mean everyone from the front desk down to your housekeepers?" Few hands went up. Yet these are people in the business of being *hospitable*.

We like to say, "It's little things that matter." I agree. And how you greet someone is a little thing that matters. It is the start of a relationship. Next time you're at your, or any, office, make a note of the greeting or the lack thereof. I find not one in ten people who can even say hello right. But if I went into any business, not just in hospitality, and said, "We are going to practice everyone saying hello," they'd say I'm nuts.

Any skill in business can be improved and developed with practice. We know this because we say it all the time—at least outside our offices. If coaches want their teams and players to get better at a sport (or a musical instrument for those non–sports players out there), what do we tell them to do? Practice! If our kids need to get better grades, what do we tell them to do? Study! We should take our own advice as business leaders. Professional athletes study routines and plays and practice them 90 percent of the time, but in business, leaders and their teams practice what they need to do less than 1 percent of the time. This is simply indefensible and violates the essential coaching principle that EVERYBODY must practice.

Let me ask you this: Do you think your team wants to work for someone, give everything they've got, and then in return get compensated and be left alone? Or would they rather work for someone who challenges them, strives to make them better by developing skills beyond their current capabilities, and helps them achieve their personal and professional goals, and the company's

Businesspeople not practicing for "game situations" are no different from athletes who do not practice: Both are unprepared.

goals as well? Put it another way: Wouldn't *you* rather have a team of that second group of people? That's the kind of person I want working for me too.

The Difference between Practice and Training

In sports, the coach's job is to make everyone better in order to put the best team on the field. To do this, coaches mandate practice and get on the field with their teams every day as they practice, working with them on the skills they need in general and specifically for the upcoming games. This should be the same for coaches in business as skill development is imperative for putting the best team "on the field." Yet too often, business leaders think product and industry knowledge can replace skill development. We may live by the rule that knowledge is power, but we forget that how well we use our knowledge determines success.

In other words, we equate a person's experience or tenure with having the skills we need to succeed. But tenure and experience can lead to complacency as often as they do betterment. They're no substitute for developing skills through practice—not training but practice. Practice is what we do on a regular basis to help us develop what we already know and get better at doing our jobs. Training is what athletes do in weight rooms and conditioning drills to get in the best possible shape for practices and games. Training is what we do in business when we are teaching employees new jobs, systems, products, or tools. In business, we tend to do the training thing pretty well, but we fall short on the practice side.

Simply put, leaders must make skill practice mandatory for everyone. No excuses. And just as for sports teams, an essential part of practice is scrimmaging. Scrimmages are safe places where we can be terrible as we work things out without fear of judgment. In fact, I wanted my teams to suck and to *learn from that*. Scrimmaging also allows coaches and teams to try something different without judgment or consequences—to get out of our comfort zones and stop playing it safe. Often we keep doing the same thing we have been doing for years, not because it is right but because it is what we know. But staying comfortable is staying complacent; it is to dwell contentedly in mediocrity.

Scrimmaging Starts with "Hello"

Scrimmaging works in all industries and for all positions, and it is a positive experience even if you are dealing with a negative subject. Planning to write up an employee? Scrimmage that. As leaders, one of the most difficult parts of our jobs is dealing with low performers. So peer scrimmage your conversation ahead of time. Discuss possible scenarios and scrimmage those scenarios. After scrimmaging the conversation with a peer, the real one might not be any easier, but it will absolutely be more successful and effective. You won't stumble and stammer at the employee's questions and end up with a to-do list for helping them instead of putting your employee on the spot to take action.

Scrimmaging conversations like these helps us avoid the traps of those situations and improves them and the skills needed to handle them. And the scrimmages can be as basic as preparing for that first greeting as someone walks into your office, store, or department. The important thing is to keep it real and focus on everyday important skills.

Here's a sample list of things you could scrimmage to help start your own coaching list for yourself and your team, many of which we cover in later chapters:

- Communicating with other teams
- Addressing conflict
- Customer service/Talking to a customer
- Never saying no
- Transferring the right energy when speaking to someone (so that person feels positive energy from the start)
- Identifying and dealing with problems
- Setting goals
- One-on-ones
- Writing
- Selling
- Presenting
- Asking purposeful business questions
- Understanding and reviewing a profit and loss statement
- Getting team buy-in
- Motivating others
- Getting out of a bad mood
- Dealing with difficult people

The key thing to remember as you make your own scrimmage list is that success comes from focusing on the most important skills for your team, not from how many different skills you work on. Start with an individual skill or two and scrimmage it every week. Attend to the basics first—the skills everyone needs and uses. This is what coaches do in sports. For example, in baseball, the entire team works constantly on the skills that make them great: hitting, fielding grounders, catching fly balls, throwing, and running. They don't practice these things because they don't know how or because game situation skills are unimportant. They practice them because they know, to be the best they can be, they must practice the basics all the time.

Leaders who get their teams to scrimmage before they do something big, such as major presentations or client calls, can also identify and deal with any mistakes that have unfortunate consequences. A major industrial distributor, one of the largest companies of its kind in the country, realized the power of practice when they struggled to answer the question, "Why us?" Why would someone choose them over their biggest competitors, the largest of which they could never compete with on price alone? To find out how they were currently answering this question, I had them scrimmage customer calls with one another and me. What I heard was every platitude in the book: We have great customer service. We *care*. We will be there when we say. We deliver under budget and on time. . . . You could make platitude wallpaper of this stuff. These sounded like the canned answers people give me in job interviews when I ask them why they want to work for me: "I'm a people person, dedicated, loyal, hardworking, and give everything I got." No one says, "I'm an unmotivated jerk and a liar and a cheat who'll be late all the time."

Practicing was uncomfortable for these construction guys. They found it annoying and weren't afraid to voice their displeasure. But their leaders forced them to keep going. After a few weeks of honest effort, the team started to listen to one another, heard the problems I did, and realized their obstacles weren't overcome by platitudes or even by pricing but specifically by what they offered better than anyone else: attention. The team thus stopped trying to compete on price, ditched the canned lines about how much they cared about their customers, and started offering details on the kind of customer attention they offered that the big boys couldn't. They talked about going on appointment calls to help contractors sell more roofs (and thus buy more product from the company) as a benefit of their experience and expertise. Soon, they were able to take what they learned in these scrimmages and walk into meetings with contractors to articulate this. The result was one of the best years the company ever had. Today, those construction guys do their practicing on their own and keep refining it based on what their customers need and on the needs of the market.

I practice what I preach too. In the course of scrimmaging phone calls to potential customers, I discovered one of my employee's greatest problems was getting past the moment someone said they were not interested in coaching and training. His response was "I'm not familiar with many companies that are successful that are not interested in training." He also told them he was "surprised" by their response. When I told him how his response made me feel (which wasn't good) in the scrimmage, he was pretty "surprised" himself. It may have sounded *to him* like a great way to overcome objections, but when he said it, I felt insulted. I felt as though he was picking a fight by challenging me, and it was creating unnecessary conflict (picking a fight like this is never good, because you can win the fight but still lose the business). After regular practice, he is now completely natural and relaxed. He says, "I get it." He relates to them and even talks about his own coaching experience. He works his way in to let them agree to send them our information and asks them simply to be open-minded about it when they get it—a much more productive approach that turned several nos into yeses.

> **Practice leads to better results—period.**

While those examples of scrimmaging are sales and customer based, leaders in *every* department and industry should know that *how* we present is as important as what is being presented. In fact, how to present is one of the most basic and essential skills to scrimmage, and you can do it yourself. I first did this at Sprint before delivering operation, or "ops," reviews when the C-suite (the CMO, CFO, CEO, et al.) came to town. Like the other division leaders, I prepared my presentation and studied my notes, but I also realized that the delivery of my ops review was just as important as my content—maybe even more important. So, in the days leading up to my presentation, I set up my camera and recorded it. Then, I would watch it not only to see how it felt to see me present but also to take notes about my performance: Where was I strong and weak? Where did I look fake? Where did I get lost or stumble over my words? And let me tell you something. It might be awkward fun watching yourself practice a presentation once, but it is miserable the second time and beyond—and powerful. Once I stopped feeling goofy and worrying about what I looked like, it was unbelievable how aware I became of everything I said. I saw the true value, and every ops review I delivered went well.

Recording yourself with a camera is the best way to scrimmage a presentation because you can see your body language as well as hear your words. But a digital voice recorder is better than nothing. If it feels strange doing that, reach out to a friend or two and offer to buy them lunch if they listen to you present as they eat and give you directed feedback after. When I worked alone, I would practice my most important presentations alone and in front of my wife, kids, and mother-in-law and tell them what to look for: Do I scream or emote too much? Does my voice inflection sound okay? Am I speaking too fast? To this day, the night before I do a speech, I am in my room going through the stories that are new as well as those I have delivered to audiences dozens of times. I do this not because I do not know them but because I want to deliver them perfectly and make sure everything I say still sounds fresh and relevant to me before I step onto the stage.

That said, scrimmaging presentations or anything else takes time to achieve the best results, and business leaders always tell me they're too busy putting out fires, returning e-mails, making client calls, and attending meetings to scrimmage as they do in sports. After all, coaches of sports teams and their players are paid to practice and coach, right? That's not only an excuse but also untrue. Most coaches in sports would argue they have just as many distractions as we do in business; they just believe there are no excuses for missing practice. So do my clients at one of the largest product manufacturers in the United States. They have even taken their practicing programs online and mandated weekly scrimmages on things like pitching on the phone. As a result, the teams have engaged the programs even further, often doing skills scrimmaging beyond the weekly sessions. Some teams have seen their results double, and all of them have learned that, as they keep getting better at what they do by practicing, they get more efficient with their time too.

The Biggest Enemy of Practice Is "We Just Hate Doing It"

I get why practice is hard: We love the "game" but not the preparation. Maybe the most fun I've ever had in sports is managing my kid's baseball games. I loved the games. On game day, I was up two hours early to have my rosters ready and think about all the in-game possibilities. But I hated doing the practices. I hated planning them, sending out grounder after grounder, explaining the drills, and repeating them time after time. Practice was often boring, for the kids and for me. I was the coach. I had to go. But the only reason those kids showed up to practice is because I made them. Business is no different. Drilling the skills and then working over and over again can be really boring. Reminding someone over and over again how you say "Hello"? That can be like nails on a chalkboard. And here is what makes it more miserable: It is the coach's job to make it lively and fun—and it has to keep being fun after the first, sixth, and hundredth week.

Truth is, no one should stop practicing until they retire or no longer desire to be the best they can be. Those who dismiss it as unimportant either hate doing it, don't understand its value, or are too arrogant to understand its importance. Anyone who wants to see a perfect, if extreme, example of this arrogance in action needs only to google "Allen Iverson Practice" and watch the former NBA star's 2002 post-game comments on practice. Iverson, one of the most prolific scorers in NBA history, had led the 76ers to the NBA Finals in 2001. This tirade happened about a year later, after the team lost in the first round of the play-offs and Iverson's coach had criticized him for hurting the team by missing practices. Iverson is both confused and frustrated by the reporters' whole line of questioning about the missed practices.

"I'm supposed to be the franchise player and we're talking about practice," Iverson rants. "Not a game, we're talking about practice. . . . How silly is that? I know I'm supposed to be there. I know I'm supposed to lead by example. . . . We're talking about practice. We ain't talking about the game. We're talking about practice. . . . We're not talking about the actual game when it matters. We're talking about practice. . . . How the hell can I make my teammates better by practicing?"

Trust me, I am not taking any of this out of context to prove a point. But please don't go throwing stones at Iverson without looking at your team and yourself first. Iverson was a supremely talented basketball player. How many of our best players do we let slide and not hold accountable for missing meetings or for thinking certain tasks are beneath them? How many people who work for us—not our worst, our *best*—if we asked them to scrimmage something, would roll their eyes and say that was crazy and dismiss it as unimportant? Are *you* rolling your eyes now?

Nobody is that good. This is plain and simple arrogance—maybe not as extreme as Iverson's but still arrogance. We would never let our kids get away with that at home or on the field. Imagine being a coach of a Little League team and one of your best players comes up to you halfway through the season and says, "Coach, I already know all these drills and skills, and I don't want

> **Without practice, all skills start to fall off—for the player and the team.**

to come to practice anymore. I'll just go to the games." What would happen if you allowed that? Your team would get worse. You would bench the kid. I don't even want to think how I would react if a coach told me it was *my* kid. It should be the same in business.

Coaches Make Practicing Exciting and Fun

Business leaders should do with practice what Emeril used to say: "Take it up a notch." Make it fast and energetic. I've done "fire scrimmaging" with entire teams to keep things moving quickly. Not ready for that? Here's one way I do it at my workshops: I pick people out of the audience to do a quick scrimmage with me as if I were a client. I stop them after two minutes and make them do it again. I stop them after one minute and say do it again. Then, I stop them and say, "Why don't you change it up and do something crazy, maybe something you are thinking about doing but would never say in a real meeting?" Then we do it again for one minute and then again, and every time, the person gets more and more confident. The audience sees this, just like your team will. And we all have fun.

This works even when I pick the surliest-looking person in the room. I was at an event for a Fortune 100 client of mine, and I spotted him right away: a middle-aged guy in hip glasses kicking back with a posture that said *Too Cool for School*. He couldn't care less about what I was saying, and he had a name like Ace or something that went perfectly with his posture. Ace was too cool to scrimmage. But sometimes the Aces can be turned into aces. Sometimes they are surly only because they want attention that they have never been given as a top performer. I usually have to work harder to get the scrimmage going, but the Aces who aren't asses will eventually step up in front of their teams. And when they do, scrimmaging becomes even *more* powerful, because Ace can now help make the *team* aces too.

Just remember your coaching principles: Everyone has to go to practice, but focus most on the top performers. Think about it. If you can improve your best two employees, how much will the entire team's results go up? While great coaches know that all their players will get better through practice, and everyone must participate, getting their top performers to practice first and do more supports a culture in which other team members strive to earn the right for more time with them. Doing the opposite—spending the most time with those who are struggling—institutes the belief that once people get to a certain level, they no longer have to practice. Better to spend the most time with top performers and have everyone trying to be in their position.

The exception to this rule is the new hire. As we will cover in more depth in Chapter 6, leaders cannot throw their new hires or "rookies" on the bench with the third string. They have to give them attention and practice with them as if they are top performers to decide quickly if they are going to make it. They deserve your attention because you've decided to bring them onto the team. Give them everything you've got to see if they go to the first string or the bench.

Yeah, We Used to Practice. . . .

And once you've got this entire practice thing going? *Keep it going.* Even when we get started practicing, we can eventually get tired of it and think, "Hey, we've done this for eight weeks and everyone has started getting a little better. So let's stop." But those eight weeks of "better" were because of eight weeks of practice. Of the hundreds of companies I have worked with on implementing a practice and skill development program, every one of them sees and believes in the benefit of skill development. But, sadly, less than *half* of those clients maintain it on a consistent basis. They don't stop because they don't believe in it; they stop because it is hard work, time-consuming, and not instantly gratifying.

For example, if a leader has seven direct reports and she wants to implement a weekly practice meeting (in place of a staff meeting) with one-on-one coaching sessions for each member, she's looking at an additional eight hours to fit into her week. Does she have those eight hours just lying around? Probably not. But she still needs to find the time and prioritize practice above almost everything else. Can you think of anything—whether a business skill, sport, or hobby—that, if you spent fifty hours a year working with a coach on, you wouldn't be better at?

Yes, coaching and skill development are redundant. Yes, practicing the same skill over and over is not new and exciting.

Yes, it is time-consuming. Yes, it is frustrating not to see immediate progress or even failure. Yes, it requires conflict and we'd rather tell people "That was good" instead of "Here's how you can make it better."

But the next time a team member is challenged to use that developing skill and is more successful, it is completely exhilarating. The harder the skill we develop, the stronger the result, and as we master skills, they become less hard to practice. A year later, I guarantee, your team will be better than they were, not just older.

Takeaways:
Skill Practice and Player Development

- Coaches must mandate practice and understand the difference between practice and training.
- What makes a business person a great asset is not experience but skill.
- Scrimmaging is the key to successful practices.
- Take the advice we give kids in sports: "Practice like you play."
- Keep scrimmaging fun, stay focused (especially on top performers), and don't give in to the urge to stop.

Chapter 2
GIVE GAME BALLS AND MVPS:
RECOGNIZE TEAMS AND INDIVIDUALS

Not everybody gets or deserves a game ball in business. There are no trophies for participation.

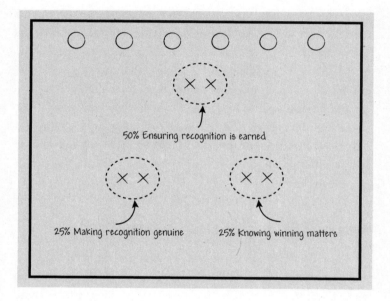

50% Ensuring recognition is earned

25% Making recognition genuine

25% Knowing winning matters

As I mentioned at the start of this book, I have been fortunate (or crazy) enough to coach my son's Little League baseball teams. And while I may know a thing or two about coaching and team building, I am no expert on the finer points of baseball. Some of those kids had much better skills than I. But a baseball coach doesn't need the skills to field a grounder or swing a bat better than the team, just the skills necessary to make the team great. Still, the tricks of this trade were not in my coaching repertoire. Knowing I needed to know what I didn't know, I went to baseball coaching clinics every year. There, I relearned a lesson from the business world in baseball terms: **Coaching is not just about the *ball*. It is mostly, and most importantly, about instilling beliefs in the team and guiding those beliefs into successful action.**

Following that clinic, I resolved to use my time as a coach to teach the boys about *life*, namely that what they believe in and how they act will affect them now, during the season, and even when they become adults. I also made sure the parents of the boys I coached had a clear understanding that this was how I was going to coach their kids. So, before every season, I had the players and parents over to my home to discuss my team "rules" for the upcoming season. The rule most parents struggled with was one I now repeat constantly as a business leader: Not everyone will receive a game ball, and some people may receive more than one during the season.

Awards and Recognition Must Be Earned

Whether it is baseball or business, unearned awards and recognition only serve to stifle motivation of top performers who receive nothing special for their excellence. Meanwhile, those who receive unearned awards and recognition know they're being undeservedly acknowledged or, worse, think what they are doing *deserves* acknowledgment! This is not just unfairness perpetrated by seemingly being fair but a failure of the coach to push *everyone* to do their best. In more than five seasons of coaching, I stayed true to my word, and not every kid received a game ball. But did that lead to mutiny in the ranks? The exact opposite: Every team member was proud of those who earned recognition and strove to earn a game ball themselves.

Today, there are a growing number of books that back up this approach. As Ashley Merryman, coauthor of *Top Dog: The Science of Winning and Losing*, wrote in *The New York Times*: "Whether your kid loves Little League or gymnastics, ask the program organizers this: 'Which kids get awards?' If the answer is, 'Everybody gets a trophy,' find another program." *Of course,* coaches should always try to find a *true* success from *every player* and acknowledge those successes, but each player still has to *earn* the bigger recognition. I wanted my Little League boys to know that a game ball is special. Business leaders should obey the same principle: Everyone deserves a chance and respect, but everybody must *earn* the "game ball." The problem is, too many leaders and organizations now do what those misguided youth sports leagues do—sacrifice rewarding those who deserve credit for excelling so as not to upset those who don't. I could not disagree more with this approach. I also 100 percent disagree that competition is unhealthy. I coach my Little League kids to be their best and play to win every game with humility and great sportsmanship. We win with modesty and lose with confidence. This is how coaches must lead their teams in business.

Simply put, leaders must appreciate every member of their team for their effort and contributions while also recognizing the specific achievements of the best performers for their excellence. So don't worry about leaving people out when awarding game balls. This recognition of success shows your gratitude and helps push people to greatness. And despite what they might say, most everybody wants, needs, and likes to be recognized and appreciated regularly. In my experience, even people who say they don't want appreciation, or have a tough time accepting it, desire it deep

Competition is good and healthy when done right.

down. Most people who say they don't need recognition, only their paycheck, are usually being humble, feeling bad for someone else on the team, or lying; everyone else is just being selfish. Saying it might also be a sign of anything from a lack of confidence to a bad attitude that needs to be confronted.

Individual Recognition Is Still about the Team

Recognizing any team member who does great things or achieves small victories becomes unhealthy only when a leader uses it to put down other members or when it becomes the defining moment within the team. It is a balancing act, but it's not terribly difficult. Recognition and reward need to acknowledge a person's performance *and* reinforce with everyone that the person is still part of a *team*. This is especially true when the members of a team work remotely or on the road and are usually out of sight. It's all too easy for those team members to feel distant and disconnected. Recognition and appreciation from the coach helps tie them to the group and pull the team together.

For example, at the gym where I work out, we cheer everyone to finish strong. The ones finishing last get the most cheers to keep them pressing forward, and the top finishers get recognition on the "leader board." The cheers are our way of showing appreciation for all without diminishing the success of the top performers. The large-scale equivalent of this in business might be offering a year-end trip or celebration for those who finish ahead of the team's individual annual goals. If done right and in a healthy way, once your top performers earn that incentive, they are still your leaders, but they have no disincentive to helping their teammates get into the spotlight and, as a result, those leaders feel less isolated and the team wins big.

But these programs do not need to involve expensive or lavish gifts. There are many small gestures with practically zero cost that can fairly recognize and appreciate an entire team without alienating the top or ignoring the bottom performers. In my first book, I told the story of the King Pin award, which consisted of passing a bowling pin award from winner to winner every week. The reward had no monetary value; it was based in pride and personal achievement. A client of mine has a fantastic method for recognizing his top performers and the successes of all team members: a bell. When I first visited him, I noticed the bell, but I didn't think to ask about it until after a few visits. He told me that when someone on the team did something great, such as set an elusive appointment, close a sale, or run a successful event, the team member would ring the bell, which sounded throughout the office. I told him how awesome that was, and he told me that it gave each person who rings it a huge sense of accomplishment as well as recognition and celebration among his or her peers. It also motivated everyone. Until it didn't.

Keep the Bell, Fire the Employee

I was so excited for my client at the time that I failed to realize *why* I hadn't asked about the bell until one of my later visits: I never heard it ring when I was there. When I asked him about this, he sighed and told me they had stopped using it recently because the team members who hadn't rung the bell in quite a while were feeling "left out and ignored." My client's intention was good (not to hurt his employees), but as a result, he removed something *great* and created a bigger problem.

"Let me get this straight," I said. "You stopped letting those who were doing a great job and striving for success ring the bell and celebrate their successes because you didn't want to hurt the people who failed to have one success worth shouting about?"

My client nodded. "Here is the problem," I continued. "People who resent the success of others will never have success themselves. You can't have people on your team who resent the recognition and success of others. You can't have people on your team who use lack of recognition as an excuse to feel bad about themselves rather than trying harder."

The right recognition creates healthy energy.

What I tried to explain to my client that day is essential to the success of any reward or recognition from bell to blowout trip: Healthy competition comes from members of the team viewing others' successes as a motivator—to learn from them and achieve. It is not nice or smart to punish those who give your team everything they have to be "nice" to those who don't. Who are you really being nice to? Acknowledging everyone is simply a misguided and selfish avoidance of conflict by the leader.

Have the Right System and Keep It Real

I have a passion for recognizing people, but more times than not, I get busy and forget to recognize those team members who deserve it. Thus, like any coach, I need systems to show appreciation and acknowledge successes. But at the same time, I have to be sure I don't make those systems so forced that they become insincere. They have to be sustained but heartfelt and informal.

I emphasize nonformality because so often when an organization devises a formal ad hoc program in which recognition is par for the course, such as a COUPON FOR BEING CAUGHT DOING SOMETHING RIGHT, it generally makes the entire process seem disingenuous and disliked by everyone. Recognition cannot be forced on people. A genuine sense of appreciation and not a forced action translates to the team's doing something because they want to, not because they have to. That's why formal, less-than-genuine recognition programs fade quickly. **That's why a genuine thank-you goes a lot further than an "on the spot" gift card that is part of a forced program.**

The bigger problem of forced formal systems is that the memory of them becomes a barrier to future genuine recognition. Team members become apprehensive of anything new, including ongoing changes to the organizational culture that leaders make when changing from managers to coaches. What is true for our employees is also true for us: Our sincerity has to be felt, and so it has to be real. Leaders can't appreciate and recognize team members by going through the motions. We have to mean it and want to do it. If either of these is absent, our employees know it.

You see this in business all the time and feel it the second you walk in the door. Once again, it all goes back to "Hello." You walk into a store and hear an unenthusiastic voice say something like, "Hello, welcome to the Dungeon of Service. How may I help you?" The words may be right, but the energy and body language tell us the employee is only going through the motions. Sometimes you want to grab these people, shake them, and say, "You should just quit, because you obviously don't like doing this job!" I have been known to do this with service people at times (minus the grabbing and shaking). And yet employees like this are not entirely to blame, because they have never received any *genuine* recognition or sincerity from their leaders and thus lack the passion and enthusiasm to show it to others.

> **If the intent is real, then the value will be real: Genuinely celebrate the small victories.**

I am not saying that formal reward systems are bad. There are times when having formal reward systems—employee of the month, top player of the month, best team player, etc.—are warranted and effective. But they are easier to implement on the sales and customer service sides of business. When it comes to factory workers, accounting, human resources, creative, and operations roles, a formal reward system becomes more difficult to maintain, and to keep everyone motivated and sustaining it can be difficult when the energy fades. So, if you're going through the motions to pick this month's MVP, it might be more prudent to ditch the formal system.

Build a Genuine Recognition System and Sustain It

Once leaders are ready to establish genuine systems for a weekly or monthly recognition program, it is essential they start by deciding what they want to recognize before they figure out what the reward is. Take the time to think it through and create it, and then don't be afraid to change it if it needs changing. The best program will develop over time, but don't wait, because it will never be perfect. The only thing more expensive than reward programs and motivating your team is doing nothing at all. Keep in mind: Our people never tell us they are discontent or bored; they show us by leaving.

Start by thinking of the tasks your most successful team member does that you could acknowledge:

- What achievements stand out among your team members who routinely go above and beyond the call of duty? List them.
- What actions of theirs make your job as leader easier? List them.

- Make a list of the actions that most and maybe all of the members of your team need to do better. What would help the team members better serve people both internal and external to the organization?

At Sprint, I was fortunate enough to work with a great finance leader, Charlie Moore. Charlie was in charge of the regional finance team for the Southeast, and I was in charge of the region's sales teams. Charlie's job was far more powerful than mine. His team was responsible for helping the company create the tools and matrix to measure our business and find ways to maximize our customer experiences, sales, and profits in ways that made financial sense. But Charlie knew authority does not make you powerful; real power comes with the ability to be valuable to others and help influence their success. And how he recognized the people who worked for him certainly influenced me.

Most finance and sales relationships are summarized as "the sales teams are there to make sales, and the finance teams are there to keep them in line." Sales and finance are almost always placed in an adversarial relationship that creates resentment—and I did jokingly call Charlie's team "The ASS [Anti Sales Support] Team." It was all in fun, though, because Charlie's formal reward system was anything but a joke and provided me with the foundation I use to guide leaders in setting up their own formal systems.

Rewards can mean nothing if the coaches are unclear about what they are recognizing.

To keep his process as objective as possible, Charlie focused on measurable achievements, those he had seen and those he'd learned about by speaking directly to partners and team leaders. Here is how Charlie formed his basis. First, he defined the attributes and actions of top players:

- Great working relationships with client partners
- Part of the solution, not part of the problem
- Happily does those tasks that don't look like his job
- Thinks outside the finance guidelines to achieve great and financially sound success
- Remains humble while operating with great confidence

Then he listed the actions everyone needed to do better:

- Be visible to client partners (get out of the office)
- Become part of the creation process so their involvement is desired
- Proactively call and meet with partners
- Constantly work to help their partners achieve their goals

Once these lists were done, Charlie was able to outline who would be rewarded and recognized each month, and his team knew exactly what they had to do. Charlie knew being a great coach meant focusing on the skills and attributes of top players, appreciating everyone every day, and recognizing excellence regularly, regardless of the reward. Genuine recognition was the point because when we coach people this way, we are making *them* better. When we just lead or manage people, we sometimes make *business* better and give people more tenure, but we're not focused on them, on their attributes and skills. Thinking about what it means to want to be appreciated can thus help us see things in a different way.

Remember: A Job Must Be More than a Paycheck

In the end, coaches understand the meaning of appreciation and how powerful a tool it can be.

A few years ago, I was talking to a good friend of mine about his job. He told me he liked his job okay, but he was growing more and more bored with it. He made great money, but he was not challenged and felt he was just going through the motions. The following year, I caught up with him after his company went through changes, and the activities and requirements of his job had changed. I asked again about his job, and he said, "I am working my tail off and traveling. I am working harder and being challenged more than ever, but I don't make any more money."

I said, "Just a year ago, you were unhappy or bored because you were not doing enough, and now you feel you are doing too much?" I was thinking, *What will make this boy happy?* But many of us are exactly like my friend in the workplace—not sure what is missing, yet knowing *something* is missing. My friend is a superstar employee for a large telecom company: hardworking, very passionate, and always willing to do what it takes to help his team and support his leadership and clients. He loves the company, and it is a great one to work for. But my friend works remotely and travels to see his clients. It is a lonely job a lot of the time, away from the team and apart from the intimate involvement and support of those he works with. He felt unappreciated and unconnected to something bigger.

Since remote offices and leadership are a way of life in most businesses, it is more important than ever that we compensate for the lack of a team environment. Concluding "it is what it is" will get us nowhere. Fortunately, my friend's new boss was a coach and understood this. He heard what my friend wanted: appreciation, respect, and, most important, to be included in something bigger. He knew my friend's need for all this would never be offset by money short-term if he continued to be unhappy long-term. And so, he made my friend come into the office and work more from there.

My friend, I'm glad to say, now loves his job more than ever. Although he at first complained of having to go to the office every day and not traveling as much, he is being challenged and he feels appreciated and recognized for his efforts and success, not only by the boss and company but by his team as well. Leaders like my friend's boss know they must nurture those who strive for great achievements and demonstrate all of the great attributes of winning team members: passion, desire, great attitude, great energy, caring, and pride in their work. That's not some feel-good, touchy-feely mumbo jumbo; it is real stuff that goes beyond the paycheck.

Takeaways:
Game Balls and MVPs

- Winning matters: Don't be afraid to recognize those who win and to appreciate the top performers.
- Rewards and recognition show appreciation for those who do great things and motivate others to strive for great things.
- Don't hurt those who give you everything to please those who give you very little.

- Implement reward and recognition to change behavior positively and sustain it—for leaders and the team.
- Be genuine in your appreciation and recognition, or don't do it at all.

Chapter 3
HAVE QUARTERLY GAME PLANS AND PEER PRESENTATIONS

Having a plan versus having a thought

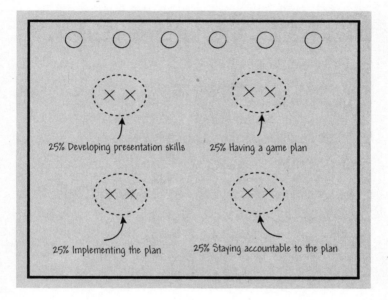

25% Developing presentation skills

25% Having a game plan

25% Implementing the plan

25% Staying accountable to the plan

Many organizations and leaders *say* they use some type of yearly or quarterly business plan. Perhaps you have one yourself in a desk drawer or on a bookshelf. Chances are you haven't looked at it since you made it. Yet every fourth quarter, most leaders do the same thing: Take last year's business plan, blow the dust off of it, change the date to the following year, update the numbers in the graphs, and call it good. Make a plan for the new year? *Check!*

Sadly, some companies are happy with this. I have seen too many leaders and teams attain consistently mediocre performance simply by not using their game plans and updating them quarterly. Imagine how successful they would be if they acted deliberately and purposefully. These plans are one of the best tools coaches have to hold their teams accountable. But at least those leaders with the dusty plans are one big step further in planning than the countless leaders out there who, if you asked to see their plan, would smile, tap their index finger to their temple, and say, "I got it right here." Imagine how successful they would be if they actually got as far as *writing* that plan. Let's clear this up right now: What they have is a thought, not a plan. They're winging it, gambling on ideas that haven't been fully realized in the most complete and effective way.

A thought becomes a plan when you write it down—when you can see it, critique it, put it into action, and revise it based on experience. Leaders might be doing okay implementing the thoughts they have without taking the time to write them out, but they're not reaching their full potential, and neither are their teams. They're not seeing all options and avenues. You can't do that with a thought or a plan sitting on a shelf for eleven months of the year. No coach can. In sports, if a coach does not prepare a game plan, write it out, *and* update it throughout the season, he is not setting up his team for success. Have you seen the size of an NFL playbook? It qualifies as weight lifting to me. Business should be the same way—maybe not in the size of the plan but in its importance to leaders and their teams. Coaches must develop and use these plans. They are *essential* to ensuring that team members regularly refocus and to measuring their success.

Think of it this way: You use some scheduling software or desk calendar, right? You don't try to remember every appointment. When you go to meetings, you take notes to remember things, scribble questions you want to ask, and maybe post something on social media when something inspires you. You want to remember it. You keep records. You make use of the written word when you're serious about documenting, studying, and remembering. Yeah, you might get there by moving from thought to action, but writing it out first makes it visible and understandable to everyone, revisable, and thus much more improvable.

Write Down Your Plan

A true game plan needs consistent reviewing, adjustments, and updates. Keep it open on your desk, computer, or portable device. Mandate your team do it as well. Inspect their game plans too: Make sure they're using theirs by using yours.

I am the first one to admit I don't like doing this. For me, writing plans—heck, writing anything—ranks right up there with root canals and colonoscopies. I love talking. I can *talk* about leadership coaching all day, every day, 365 days a year. However, even I admit that my talking improves when I write down ideas, look at them, and pass them on to others for review. Writing down my ideas enables me to be intentional about what I say and what I do. I'm not winging it from my brain. I know where I'm going and how I'm going to get there because I've planned my route . . . and then I plan it again and again.

> Without a game plan, all leaders end up doing is reacting.

The enemy of an effective game plan is the set of excuses leaders make as reasons why composing a detailed game plan would be a waste of our time: "I already do what I need to do" or "I have it on my iPad to-do list" or "I've been doing this job for twenty years, so I know all I need to know." Perhaps my favorite excuse is "My schedule changes every day and too much to plan so far ahead." When it comes to our excuses, we sound no different from our kids. I know what would happen if my son's school did not have a set schedule but just told him to attend English, math, economics, and Spanish and make sure he grabbed lunch. My son is a great kid and he would have every intention of going to class, but chances are he would miss everything but lunch. We have to make ourselves overcome the equivalent as leaders. We need to either plan our actions and let *others* react or spend our time unplanned and get lost reacting to others' actions.

Remember the Difference between a Game Plan and a "Set of Results"

When I ask to see a client's business plan, I usually get a list of sales, budget, production, safety, and other goals. These "plans" and the results they hope to achieve are not game plans but summaries of objectives. Goals and objectives should comprise a part of any game plan, but they cannot be the entirety of that plan. This would be the equivalent of the coach of a football team tossing aside his playbook and saying, "We want to score points and win the game. We want to keep our players healthy and protect the quarterback and play great defense and thus win as many of these games as we can and make the play-offs. Then, we want to go to the Super Bowl and win!"

"Okay," the team would say. "But *how?*" That "How?" is the question the game plan is supposed to answer. **A true game plan notes the activities and plays you will need to execute to reach your objectives.** It tells the team what they are going to do to achieve their goals, and how and when they are going to do it. Here, for example, are what a couple of short game plans might look like for a plant manager.

- What: Walk the plant floor.
- When: 4 times per day (8 A.M., 11 A.M., 2 P.M., 5 P.M.)
- How: Inspect, assist where needed, point out superstars, interact with each team member, give direction as needed.

- What: Conduct one-on-one meetings with team supervisors.
- When: Once per week (Set it on the calendar at the beginning of each month.)
- How: During my weekly meetings, discuss performance of the teams. Discuss any leadership or personnel issues. Spend 10 minutes on personal growth.

Now, a real game plan for this plant manager should be more in-depth, with more detail about the activities that include time allocations and content, but at the same time, it does not need to fill a three-ring binder just for show. It should be a manageable document that is consulted weekly, if not daily. If printed, it should be covered with coffee stains and ink from constant morning review.

Mandate the Team to Keep Game Plans Current and Focused

After creating a game plan, coaches must keep it in play and updated. Like sustaining skill practice and recognition programs, this is always a bigger challenge than creating the program. This is where leaders can bring their teams in to help. I have found that the only way I have been able to keep my plan relevant and in play is by requiring my team to do it. Doing this holds them accountable and holds me accountable as well. Too many leaders don't mandate their people to do this because then *they* would have to do it—a legitimate concern but not a good one.

How, in practice, do you mandate the use of a game plan? Incorporate it in your one-on-one meetings with your team. Use it on the day you plan your next week. If you are thinking that you don't have the time to review your plan in preparation for the next meeting, then start your game plan there! Leadership in most businesses does not have a daily structure. In most companies, it is up to the leader to coordinate the key activities to create a structure. So do that and make it a part of the game plan. After that, add the specific tasks you need to be doing to grow your business and your team.

We will do only what we are held accountable to do.

Recently, I was conducting a "preparation call" with a new client in the shipping and transportation industry. I spend about an hour on these calls, asking everything about their organization, people, key activities, and goals. That way, I can get the best understanding of their culture and make my presentation customized and relevant to their specific business. During this particular call, I asked my client to describe the perfect day and week of activities for a person in such-and-such a role. "Tell me as if I were a robot and I would do exactly what you want and need me to do to be the best at that position," I said.

Here was her answer: "You would go on five client meetings a week and conduct five meetings with the GM in charge of those locations and meet with the number one producer of each office. Next, I would expect you to go on four joint calls with our field agents. I would also expect that the agents view you as a great enough value to have invited you to go to these meetings with them. Last, you would be in your office doing administrative stuff only one day per week. Most of your time would be in the field with your team and clients."

"Perfect," I said. "Now tell me what is happening in the real world."

"Well the top ten percent of our team members are doing these activities, and most of them are doing much more. About fifty percent are fulfilling half of these expectations. The rest are doing about ten percent of the expected activities."

"Why are most of them not doing what you expect?" I asked. That was the question they wanted me to answer, but my call had already revealed what it was. Why does any company like this tolerate employees who do not do the expected activities? The answer is a lack of accountability.

Having our team members create, use, and update game plans is a great way to hold our teams and us accountable to them. Here is the big-picture view of how this works in my business:

- I give my team members expectations that include all key activities I believe are imperative for their success.
- In my expectations for the team, along with expected activities, I also provide expected results.
- The team members in turn create their own personal game plans for how they are going to exceed my expectations.
- We review their game plans and make sure we

both agree that it makes sense and will generate the best possible results. (By saying we both agree means we don't go below my minimum expectations, and the plans are pushing them outside their comfort zone.)

- Once we have agreed and all necessary changes have been made, it becomes our law, our personal commitment, and the overall map to our success.

My game plans are the documents each person on my team will be held accountable for every day, week, month, quarter, and year. It is now also *their* document—one they have ownership of and not one that was given to them by corporate or by me playing Moses. They have created and committed to doing it. This is basic business ethics—doing what you say you will do. So all I am asking of my team members is that they be ethical.

Quarterly Plans Make Accountability Better at the Top and Bottom

Without fail, every time my team and I do our plans, my top performers, or soon to be top performers, exceed my expectations regarding activities and results. If I ask them to do five of something, they will commit to eight and then perform ten. If I ask them for $1,000 in revenue, they will commit to $1,200 and then perform to $1,500. Logical thinking, which we will cover in the next chapter, keeps growing and growing.

And without fail, every time we do our plans, my bottom performers try to justify why the expectations regarding activities and results are unrealistic or too high. None of their reasons are based on their own ability or lack of desire. It is always someone else's fault or the company's fault. This might reveal something as serious as a latent case of victim disease (see Chapter 8) or a lack of commitment. Or it might help leaders address a problem we did not see, such as a misunderstanding of the goal and the reasons behind the business plan. Whatever the cause for the excuses, I have found it best to address them up front. This way, the team members have time to rethink their commitment, rethink their desire to be in their position, or rethink what they did not understand so there are no more misunderstandings on my part or theirs.

I remember reviewing one of my team member's business plans with him and discussing his committed activity and results. He was experienced and knowledgeable about the business but lacked a sense of urgency and desire to get better and really strive for more. He told me that my expectations were unrealistic and offered several reasons why. I let him share all of his concerns, perceived obstacles, and excuses with me. In fact, I acknowledged that many of his points were fairly accurate. But we get paid to make business happen, not to sit back and wait for things to happen because things are out of our control. I shared with him all of the reasons why and how we needed to overcome the obstacles—both real and merely perceived. I wanted him to hear from me that I was more concerned with how he responded than with the issues in his response. So I told him all of this.

I said, "Mr. X, I am most concerned that you truly believe these expectations cannot be met, given our current situation, and that you are unwilling to do the following expected activities from our plan to achieve our goal. I respect and appreciate your honesty and sharing, so I want to make sure I give you the same openness and honesty as well. At the end of the day, we get paid to overcome obstacles and not to accept any excuses. These activities *have* to be met and the results will follow, but only if they are done with the passion and drive to get them done. I am concerned that you will be unable to accept this plan and lead your team with these initiatives."

Then, I turned to the game plan we had developed and continued, "You are correct that these expectations are hard and will require change and a large commitment, and that is what we need from everyone, including you. I need you to go think through this game plan and decide if this is something you can believe in and choose to do without hesitation. If not, I understand and respect your appraisal of the situation and your abilities. With that being said, we may need to make a decision about where you go next. I would be more than happy to find a better fit for your attributes and skills, whether it is inside the organization or outside the organization."

The next day, Mr. X came into my office and told me he was "in" and willing to do everything he could to meet my expectations. Problem is, he thought this was what I wanted to hear. It wasn't. I wanted to hear him declare his commitment to the game plan and deliver on it and then exceed my expectations. Without considering the game plan in front of us, Mr. X's words were empty, which is what too many leaders have—empty pages to hold people like Mr. X accountable to.

With the plan on the table, Mr. X and I both knew he had no real intention of implementing it; we both knew he would never be accountable for it. Within six weeks, Mr. X secured a position outside the company that would better fit his goals and aspirations, and I was able to put a new passionate and committed team member in his place. In less than six months, the team was on track to set new records.

Presenting Plans Peer to Peer, Not Just Coach to Team, Increases Accountability

Just as teammates need to get used to scrimmaging skills and activities, I am a huge believer that teams also should present their business plans in front of their peers and coaches whenever possible. So, once coaches and teams have created their game plans, agreed to the game plans, and talked about the importance of holding teams accountable for the game plans, it is then time to discuss *presenting* the game plan. There are lots of little reasons for this, but the three biggest reasons are the most important:

- Group accountability
- Sharing best practices
- Developing presentation skills

Group accountability

When we present in front of our peers and make personal commitments, we are more likely to do what we committed to do. I encourage the groups to get involved and even to call BS when they see it—not to humiliate or hurt their peers but to help and challenge them to be better. There is no hiding from the accountability once they are finished, either. My team members who participated in quarterly peer reviews knew that, in ninety days, we would be standing in front of one another explaining how we did compared to our commitments. This not only empowers the team to be accountable to one another but also takes some of the accountability pressure off the coach's shoulders in the best way.

Sharing best practices

It is one thing to exceed expectations; it is another to learn what they mean over the long term. Peer-to-peer presentation sessions have the power to shatter expectations of what cannot be done, because team members not only hear how fellow members achieved what others said could not be done but also hear about the benefits of doing so. This leads to encouragement, motivation, and, perhaps, the fuel of healthy competition, pushing lower performers to reach the top, and top performers to get better and exceed expectations in order to stay ahead. This is why sharing best practices is usually the most boisterous and favorite part of each person's presentation. It gives everyone a chance to shine, feel good, and share things that are working.

Developing presentation skills

Public speaking is one of the greatest fears in business today. Peer-to-peer presentations overcome this in a way that goes beyond scrimmaging to build confidence and personal growth top to bottom. I was working with a client conducting peer reviews when one of the most experienced employees had the worst presentation. His content and activities were great, but his presentation was dry. His body language was so poor, you would have thought he hated his job—yet he spoke and did small presentations inside and outside the organization on a regular basis. . . . Yikes! When I asked my client if he was surprised by the person's presentation skills, he said, "Yes, I am shocked. I thought he would have done better than that since he presents in his job."

Over the next several months, during one-on-one meetings and special time set aside, we scrimmaged this employee's presentation skills. The next presentation, ninety days later, showed incredible improvement. He prepared more and did not read the slides; instead, he told a story and used the slides as a guide. He was engaging and entertaining. The conversations about this employee's performance were initially difficult, but after a year of peer reviews and ongoing coaching, this employee believed in himself and felt more confident in what he does—and it showed.

Of course, like many things that are good for us, there is a cost to conducting peer reviews of our game plans. Peer reviews, like the plans themselves, sometimes fall prey to the "power of the new," gaining traction at first but wandering from the road and fading from view soon after. They get removed from the key activities list because they take time (assuming each person has up to forty-five minutes to present). For coaches and their teams, it can be a beatdown to sit there and listen to everyone's presentation, but it is a *beneficial* beatdown. Trust me: **The rewards of everybody having a renewed focus every three months through peer-to-peer game plan presentations make up for the couple of days in preparation and the couple of days in presenting.**

Think of how fast your business changes—weekly, even daily in some cases. Are quarterly adjustments and updates really too frequent? Isn't having a game plan that is more than something that sits in a three-ring binder gathering dust on a shelf, but instead raises the accountability level of the entire team, going to help you win better and more? Every team in sports needs a game plan to compete and win. Remember: Creating it is just the beginning. We must use it and present and share it for optimal results.

Takeaways:
Quarterly Game Plans and Peer Presentations

- The only thing worse than an ignored or bad game plan is no game plan—if it is not written down, it's a thought, not a plan.

- Game plans can be a time-consuming beat-down, so while they are extremely important, they get done only when a leader or coach mandates them.
- Don't stop reviewing your plans, no matter how busy your team becomes or how repetitive the reviews.
- Peer presentations are tough, time-consuming, and sometimes inconvenient, but the rewards are HUGE for presentation skills, focus, best-practice sharing, accountability, and success.

Chapter 4
SET LOGICAL, NOT REALISTIC, GOALS

Take the power out of the past and strive for what can be done, not what has been done.

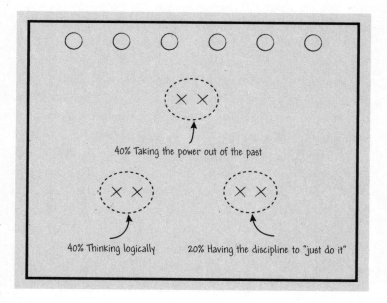

40% Taking the power out of the past

40% Thinking logically

20% Having the discipline to "just do it"

Why do the best coaches in sports always have the confidence of the owners and players that they can win, and even win it all every year—although they don't win it all every year? Because *no one* wins it all every year. They do win and lose championships and have great overall won-lost records, but that is irrelevant. The best coaches don't rest on their past laurels. They celebrate the achievement and then have the ability to forget the past and use it for experience rather than as a forecaster. They reevaluate everything each season, beginning anew with revised game plans and the logical belief that their teams can beat the other teams every time.

It doesn't matter what those coaches' teams look like on paper or that "experts" in the media are telling them it is not realistic. It is not about setting realistic goals. It is about thinking *logically*. Being logical simply means that given enough time, commitment, and skill, that team *could* win every game and win it all. Has it been done in the modern era? Once or twice. So is it possible? Yes. And now, even if a star player gets hurt and they lose a game or miss the post-season, those coaches' teams still have winning attitudes that make for great teams, seasons, championships, dynasties, and winning cultures people want to play for and fans want to see year in and year out.

It should be no different for leaders who are coaches in business. In business, being logical means believing that some team or company has to be number one, so why not mine? Leave the realistic goal setting for finance and making budgets. Being realistic almost everywhere else limits us to the standards of past achievements. Realistic goals too easily keep us tied to what's been done. They are inhibitors that lead to playing it safe. They say that dreams are only real when we are sleeping. So out those dreams go. Logical goals propel us into the future, and leaders must push their teams to dream big, not just to win but to attain what has never been attained—and to believe they can do this.

Unfortunately, most leaders are taught to set "realistic" goals, using some version of the acronym SMART (Specific, Measurable, Attainable, Realistic, Timely) to define what those goals are. I even used SMART goals in my previous book. I still think it is a useful acronym for realistic thinking, but today my

A realist is only a pessimist in denial.

SMART goals for coaches are a little *smarter*: Specific, Measurable, Attainable by me, Relevant, and Timely.

Replacing *Realistic* with *Relevant* in SMART is easy enough to understand. It eliminates the realistic mind-set but reminds us to keep our thinking from being impossible and irrelevant to our business. But in that small variation of *Attainable* to *Attainable by Me* is an essential difference between realistic and logical thinking—not confusing *attainable* with *having been attained*. Logical goal setting challenges us to be the best and break records. If coaches set only the goals for their teams that have been attained by others, records would never be broken. Usain Bolt, Michael Phelps, and Lindsey Vonn don't go to the Olympics thinking about just winning and maintaining their success. They want to be their best and set new standards. Obstacles be damned. Great coaches, players, and teams always believe they can win every game in the regular season regardless of where and when they are playing, regardless of the weather or the opponents. Whether leaders are in charge of several teams across a multinational corporation or a business of one, selling shoes or sheet metal, leading a creative team of designers or a brainy crew of engineers, **your business can logically be on top of something, so chase the logical goals.**

Action Speaks Louder than Words

We brush our teeth every morning and every night (well, I hope we all do). How can we get this way with goal setting? I don't think anybody would disagree that setting goals of any kind is important. In fact, I think most of us *want* to set goals on a daily, weekly, quarterly, and annual basis, but somehow, or for one reason or another, we don't get it done. How many times do we have to read it in a book until we actually *do* it?

I spent more than twenty-five years in corporate America. I have owned four companies. I am the father of four children. *I teach, coach, and write books about goal setting.* And yet I still consistently find myself not setting and managing my goals! My biggest struggles in logical goal setting are no longer a lack of knowledge of how to set them or the scale from realistic to logical but the discipline to *do* it. In fact, I am going to stop writing right now so we can all set three goals for this week. I will be right back. Please hold. . . .

That's a first step to making logical goal setting a priority: writing it down. Now, schedule time to do it. Start by making it a recurring meeting on your calendar, with an alert to remind you when it is coming. That's the next step, but it is not going to be enough. We know that just because it is on our calendar doesn't mean we will do it. Heck, just look at the other recurring scheduled tasks we don't do already. So how do we keep this from being a calendar cleanup item in six months? Have the discipline to keep the team and yourself focused on those goals so you start to *see* the results.

Simply put, the short-term pain of doing something that is good for us is worth it if we get the great results we need from doing it. It is like exercise and dieting. We exercise and stay on diets not because we don't want to eat cake but because we see the benefit from doing (or not doing) these things. Usually, we also have some larger goal in mind. The bigger that goal, the harder we need to work and stay focused on it to make any diet work: Is it realistic that I can lose twenty-five pounds before my college reunion in a month even though I have never dieted before? Probably not, but it is *possible* if I *want* to do it. Seeing the first pounds come off inspires me, but there are still weeks and pounds to go, and keeping the goal all in my head is not helping. Hiring a great personal trainer who shares my goal is like having a coach to push me. Telling my friends what I am doing provides support, and as Weight Watchers has shown, having a community around me that is after the same or similar goals helps me even more to sustain the work necessary to achieve my goals. The same can be said for setting logical goals for our teams and ourselves as business leaders.

Logical versus Realistic Goal Setting

Logical goal setting is of course easier to articulate when a department or team is responsible for or measures success in numbers. In sales, let's say my company's industrywide total market share is $100 million. My company has a 10 percent market share or $10 million in sales. My three top competitors have $20 million in sales or a 20 percent market share. The realist in me says, "We did ten million dollars in sales last year, and I think this year we're good to grow ten percent, twenty percent at the outside, to eleven million dollars for a market share increase of one to two percent." I got sleepy just reading that sentence.

Make logical goals important for everyone and it will be important for everyone.

The logical leader in me says, "We did ten million dollars last year and it is a hundred-million-dollar industry, and if three of my competitors can have twenty percent market share, then so can we, right? So there is no reason we can't double our sales, because they're buying the other thirty million dollars from someone else." That may not be realistic, but it is logical. Logically, I know that the other 90 percent of the market is buying from somebody else and 30 percent is buying from companies smaller than my company. I can believe that, given the number of opportunities and resources available, my company should be able to increase market share to 20 percent, the only questions being how and when.

Measurable numbers do not have to be dollar based. In Chapter 5, I talk about a leader who is in charge of safety at a dozen plants for a major manufacturer and how I used the logical goal of zero accidents in a quarter to motivate his team. Most companies say they want to have the best customer service, so how about a goal of being number one in service and reliability in your industry or market? Remember: Numbers are not just about sales, and sales aren't only about sales teams. Sales numbers are about *revenue*. Yet every time we think of revenue, volume, profits, and growth, we think, "That's just about sales." But that's not true. Revenue, growth, and sustainability are for leaders and teams in every part of a company, whether they are in creative, editorial, marketing, engineering, technology, production, or design.

Trust me, the sales departments don't think they can do it without the leaders of other departments thinking logically too. How else will a business innovate or address the needs of the customers? Sales people don't design and produce the phones, cars, computers, and kitchen equipment they are selling. They don't build the websites and program the software. They may anticipate what their customers need and innovate how they sell, but they can't innovate what they are selling or sell what the market will need three or five years from now. Five years ago, GPS devices were everywhere and salespeople were selling them like crazy. Not now. Today, more and more people use their phones for navigation, so people at Garmin better have been thinking months and years before today about adapting and designing what it could sell next lest they end up like RIM and its BlackBerry and get left behind.

The Biggest Difference between Crazy and Genius Is Success

You might think my logical goals are crazy, yet when I reach those goals (and someone can because the logical *is* possible), passing the realistic goal in pursuit of my logical goal, I'm a "genius." What do you need to be logical rather than realistic? A little crazy and a lot of belief. Was it realistic in 1994, when Barnes & Noble and other chains boomed, that Jeff Bezos wanted to build the biggest bookstore on the Internet? Should we tell our finance manager not to dream big and live big and reach her goal of becoming a CFO someday? My friend is a drummer who said all his life, "I'm going to be a drummer for one of the biggest bands in the world." Do I tell him, "Dude, that's not realistic" or, when I see him working so hard to get there, encourage his dreams? (By the way, he's now the drummer for country superstar Jason Aldean.)

Sure, it doesn't hurt to be a little naïve and not know that something can't be done or that conventional wisdom says something can't be done. When I wrote and decided to self-publish my first book, *The Sales Leaders Playbook,* in 2008, I was excited to make it a bestseller but quickly found out that writing the book was the easy part (which is saying a lot for me). *Selling it* was much harder. Still, I didn't know that or even care. With unbridled optimism, I called bookstores and distributors around the country, asking them if they would want to sell my books. I was shocked to find that they did not really care to do so. They apparently didn't hear my ego screaming at them the way it screamed at me.

I could have given up, but I didn't. I had coached myself to write out my goals and to stay focused on them, and since I travel a lot, one of my goals was to see my book in an airport bookstore.

After making too many calls to count, sending out hundreds of books, and getting more rejection than I did from girls during my high school years, it seemed that it wouldn't happen. But I soldiered on, determined to see my dream come alive. I have since discovered that most people in publishing think this is impossible without bestseller status or paying for shelf space, but back then, all I thought was, *There are books in those stores that aren't bestsellers or by well-known authors. Why not mine?*

After several months and many tries, I met a young man stocking a bookstore and I told him who I was and what I wanted to do. He had great energy and said, "My name is Rico, like Rico Suave," and we talked briefly. He told me that he would talk to his boss and see what he could do. Rico did not disappoint. After weeks of communications, meetings, and calls, we were able to get my book placed in the Dallas/Fort Worth airport. The picture of the display of my book in that first of many airport stores still sits on my "vision board" in my office, not to remind me of how far I have come but to inspire me to keep pushing the logical bar higher. My next goal is to sell a million books. People have, you know. Why not me?

Don't Use Experience to Predict the Future

Our goals must not limit us; they must challenge us. But we can't fake any of it. We have to believe that we have the *ability* to win—to be number one or achieve whatever our logical goal is. Leaders and their teams must forget the past and then believe in the goals, align themselves with those goals, and do all the activities from scrimmaging to recruiting the best players and beyond to get there.

When I took over the Southern California market for Sprint, it was among its worst-performing markets in the country. So, naturally, I told my team at the first managers' meeting that our logical goal was to be number one in sales *and* decrease our budget expenses to the lowest in the country. I told them how, to get there, we were going to implement a coaching program and culture similar to the one in this book. I explained how I would work with everyone on scrimmaging and peer presentations and coach them to

> **Just because it has never been done doesn't mean it can't be done.**

overcome any existing obstacles and to believe in our new broader vision for success.

That's when one manager stood up and said something like "Hey, you know what, I get it. The whole big-Texas-attitude-we're-going-to-make-things-happen. But, Nathan, that is not possible here!"

"Okay, why?" I asked.

"The facts are real simple," he said. "We have too many stores in this market and more competitors than you are used to, and in many cases, our competitors are better than we are. There is just too much for this team to handle already. We have never been number one, but we are pleased with where we are."

I like to call this manager the Snowman because of the snow job he was trying to sell me. This was the most cynical, pessimistic kind of thinking, and what was worse, he was playing me for the fool. He wasn't being sarcastic. He was being manipulative. He started with a backhanded compliment about my Texas attitude working in smaller markets, but he was trying to deflect me from digging deeper. He didn't want me pushing the team to overcome any obstacles. The Snowman was not a bad person, but he was using every obstacle, realistic thinking, and past experience as excuses for a lack of achievement. The Snowman was so busy believing that we were where we were supposed to be in the market that he refused to believe anything else was possible, and that prevented him from holding himself or anyone accountable. He believed it didn't matter what we did, and that the situation wasn't going to change, so why try to be better?

I had no interest in making this "okay" for the Snowman or the team. So, in this case, I came back hard at the Snowman with a speech that was partly about the power of thinking logically and partly ultimatum. I took a deep breath: "That attitude does not work for us anymore. If you think it can't be done, then it can't be done. Let's use the experience of the past to understand what our obstacles are, but let's push ourselves to reach bigger goals. The number of stores is immaterial. We have a low market share, and if people are buying phones but not buying *our* phones, we need to find out why. The issue isn't the market or our competitors. The issue is *us*. We need to find a way to be better. If anyone does not believe we can be the best, then go work for the company that is, because I want to work for the team that wants to be the best. Someone has to be number one, so why not us, together, as a team? If you can't get behind this, the company will find other people who can."

> **If your people DON'T think they can beat "them," then they should go join "them."**

The Snowman had no snow job to answer this. Neither did any of the other managers who refused to align with our goals. Of course, I wasn't this blunt with all of them, and I did give all of them time. I spent months trying to coach them to be top performers and reach our logical goal. But in the end, we terminated the Snowman and about thirty others in the office—30 percent of my team—in the first eight months.

And the Snowman was proven wrong. Once we faced the tough decision to get rid of people like the Snowman and the victims who blamed everyone but themselves for their lack of success and were not going to change, the others began to see the possibility of what we could accomplish. They started to see the market change. We didn't just improve sales, communication, and relationships at the stores; we *expanded* from thirty local retailers to sixty. Every month, as sales increased, the team's belief got a little stronger. Within eighteen months we, as an entire team, were able to achieve our goal of becoming number one and becoming one of the company's most effective and efficient markets in the country.

Not only did logical thinking turn the team around at Sprint; it made the work fun. They were actually volunteering to pass out donuts to customers at four A.M. on the day after Thanksgiving for the door-buster early bird specials—and having a blast doing it. They were working to prove something and keep winning.

As we achieved our goals, one of the managers came up to me and said, "Nathan you have to be the most unrealistic manager I have ever had. But I never have achieved so much success." He told me he initially resented me for being what he saw as unrealistic. He said he might not appreciate all the change or like it when it was happening, but he appreciated it when it was over and we saw the results of our hard work. Doing your best is never easy and takes you out of your comfort zone. Your job as a leader is to expand your team's comfort zone. When you are winning, it is the greatest pain in the world.

Can't Pitch a Strike Unless You Show Up at the Game

My wife and I tell our kids not to let anyone determine their success. We tell our kids all the time that they can do anything they want. When they are trying to do something and say, "I

can't," my wife or I will immediately respond, "You can do anything you set your mind to if you believe you can and do the
hard work to get there."

I know we are not an anomaly. Most parents tell their children this and truly believe it. Yet when it comes to our successes
as adults, especially in business, we don't believe it. And it is not
just the Snowmen making excuses, with comments like "We
can't do that because of our marketplace." It is people who just
don't believe that they or their businesses can compete on a
higher level than they already are. We say, "We can't compete
with them" or "I can't change industries because I am too old"
or "This is all I have ever done. . . ."

All the fear of failure or the worries about steep learning
curves or the hard work it will take to get to goals that we say
and believe our kids can overcome, we use to dash our own
dreams as adult professionals. So to whom are we lying? Are we
lying to our kids when we tell them they can do anything or are
we lying to ourselves when we say we can't? I have asked this
question of literally thousands of business people, and 100 percent of the time, they say that they are *not lying to their kids*—
they really believe they can do anything in life.

So, then, we are lying to ourselves when we make excuses for
inaction or for not doing any better than we already are. We
constantly tell ourselves and say out loud, "It's impossible." Well,
to paraphrase a famous line from the movie *The Princess Bride*:
We keep using that word but it does not mean what we think it
means. In fact, many things we make excuses for in business are
possible, and leaders who want to be coaches must push their
teams to understand what this really means and elevate their
success *beyond* the possible to a level that may have seemed impossible. They do this by setting goals that are logical, not just
realistic.

Takeaways:
Set Logical, Not Realistic, Goals

- Realistic goals are based on our past and are limited by our experiences; logical goals are based on what can be done based on time, capacity, and commitment.

- Make it important and it will be important: Goal setting is a benefit. Everyone agrees, yet most of us keep talking about it and don't do it, so just do it!

- Logical thinking and dreaming big is not just for kids and sales teams trying to make their numbers—they are for every leader and team that desires to get the most out of work and life!

- We believe our kids can be anything they want to be in life and yet we think we can't change careers or be number one in business because we haven't done it before. Whom are we lying to?

Chapter 5

TAKE RESPONSIBILITY FOR MOTIVATION AND MORALE

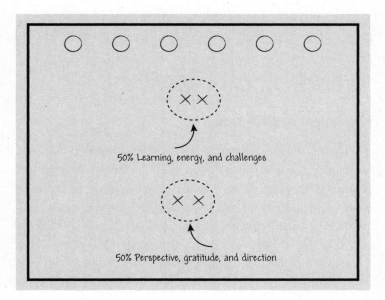

Whatever you've heard about it being a leader's job to manage, not motivate, is another lingering legacy of the management culture and the belief that a leader should hire great people and get out of their way. A leader might even say, "It's their job to motivate themselves. I pay them for that." To this and every other excuse leaders make for not motivating their teams—to every leader who says motivation does not work or can't be sustained—I say, "Baloney." No matter what anyone says, it is the leaders' job to motivate their teams.

In sports and in business, it is the coaches who must make

sure they have motivated teams who want to win. Don't get me wrong: Coaches can't do it all. I want my teams to inspire one another, and I expect a willingness to be motivated and some self-motivation too—but not at the expense of silence from me. I expect and mandate that leaders do the same: Motivate their teams with focus and discipline, passion and belief. And we must find a way to do this, not once or twice or whenever we see a cool "team bonding" exercise to try out but on a daily, weekly, and monthly basis, and then start all over again.

Motivation Leads to Action

How many times have you led a terrific meeting to rally the team in which everyone gets pumped and unites around the plan or goals being set, only to see the energy fade by the next week? This is some of the "evidence" leaders use to say this "motivation stuff" doesn't work or works only for a short time and then fades away. But that's an excuse. Motivation *does* work; it works like food in our bodies. Think about the best meal you ever had and how happy and full you were afterward. If you did not eat again for three days, would you not feel hungry? Would you think that "food stuff"

Motivation is easy to start, hard to sustain.

----

did not work? Like food for our bodies, leaders must refuel their teams with motivation and find ways to feed their teams this fuel daily. But the unfortunate truth is, most of us can't, don't, and won't get this motivated to motivate because *the job is never done.*

That's why motivation doesn't work: It needs a system to keep it going—a focused plan with which leaders must get involved, to implement with key activities and desired results on that daily, weekly, and monthly basis. Some of this plan can be achieved through the rewards and recognitions we discussed in Chapter 2. Some of the activities can be easy, such as remembering to offer kind words or brief guidance during scrimmaging and before and after a presentation. But the best ideas come from learning what is possible, believing that it is possible, and challenging ourselves to think bigger.

I was coaching an executive in charge of twelve plants throughout the United States and Canada for a major manufacturing client. One of our first discussions was about the plants' safety ratings, which were based on the number of injuries at the plants. Every quarterly plan update, he would set a goal to have a small decrease in reported injuries.

"Why not just make the goal zero?" I asked.

"Nathan, you don't get it," he laughed. "That's not possible."

We talked some more and he told me how some plants had more than two injuries and others had none. So I asked, "If one plant can have zero, then so can everybody else, right?"

"Yes, in theory, but not in reality," he said.

To his credit, the executive seemed uncomfortable with his answer. Part of his discomfort, as you might have guessed, was that he had set a realistic goal, not a logical one. He definitely knew it was *possible* to achieve those safety results. But there was something more: He knew logical goal setting and making the teams believe in it was only part of the solution; he needed a plan that would motivate the teams to achieve those goals.

He started by looking at what it would take to get the number of injuries to zero, and he created new programs and incentives to make his people better. Then, he started a program that had never been done before, implementing new ideas that he and his leadership team created. They brought together a group of peers, leaders, managers, and personnel who went to one plant at a time to do a "deep dive" into the operations and then shared the good and bad of what they found. At each plant, they found positive factors they could implement at other plants, and negative factors that needed to stop. But the team now had suggestions for improvement based on what they had learned in their travels to other plants. His program became a nationwide initiative.

Next, the plant executive also started searching for programs and ideas *outside* the company and industry and eventually mandated "plant walk-arounds," during which a plant manager walks the plant floor a couple of times a day to talk and work with the employees and supervisors. Prior to these walk-arounds, plant managers could go days or even a week before they spent time on the floor working with the team. Three quarters of consistent safety rating improvements later, the plant executive's team had achieved an all-time low in safety scores. Maybe zero injuries across the board wasn't always possible, but making his people strive for that goal motivated them to be better.

Learning, Energy, Challenges

There are many ways to motivate people, but as my plant executive's plan reveals, coaches in business can always rely on three things that almost anyone responds to: **Learning**, **Energy**, and **Challenges**.

Learning

Knowledge + Learning + Confidence = Motivation. This is the magic formula leaders must remember. Knowledge alone does not lead to motivation; learning more and in the right way builds on that knowledge and helps us get better at what we do. When we learn something valuable, we become more confident in ourselves, and as a result, we are more motivated to take action. We then keep working on what we learned and strive to learn more. That's the number one variable that determines winning or losing: confidence. The more we teach our people as coaches and hold them accountable to that learning, the more confidence they have, the more motivated they are to work, and the more desire they have to keep learning and to start the process over again.

> Challenges make you go bigger.

For the plant manager, learning what was going right and wrong at one plant and then taking the knowledge to the others to solve problems throughout all the plants made every plant better and gave his team and himself confidence to sustain the program. It also gave him confidence to look outside the industry for new ideas, which led to the idea of plant walk-arounds. Don't have a manufacturing plant you're responsible for? The essential ways for any leader to motivate through learning is to sustain the weekly and monthly practice sessions and peer presentations we covered in chapters 1 and 2.

Energy

Want your team to have the right energy? Then have it yourself and make sure your team can feel it in what you say and, more important, what you do. It's not just paramount that coaches genuinely believe in all the principles of coaching and that they follow the actions of their playbooks—they must be passionate about them. We have spent a considerable amount of time discussing the bad attitudes on a team and how it brings a team down, but **leaders must remember that their positive attitudes and the energy that comes from them can motivate the team to find solutions to overcome obstacles**.

Positive energy—fueled by passion for the job and the success of the team—will motivate any team to success; negative energy—fueled by a lack of passion—will motivate the team to fail. The walk-arounds of the plant manager engaged the employees and transferred his positive energy to the teams on the floor, motivating them to do more to succeed. They wanted to get better now too. This can't happen in the four walls of leaders' offices. It is imperative for us to remember our coaching principles and get involved with our teams. We'll cover getting "on the field" with the team in more detail in Chapter 12, but for now, remember to smile, share your passion with the team, and engage your top performers positively.

Challenges

Like top-performing athletes, top-performing teams don't just want to be coached; they want to be challenged. When they are given a larger area of responsibility, they view the increase as a compliment—a sign that their bosses believe in them and their capabilities—and are motivated to do more.

It is easy to see how the plant manager challenged himself not only with logical goals but also by going outside the industry and doing things no one had attempted before. A simple way of implementing this in any office is to use a basic challenge model that does not need to be connected to rewards and recognitions: Every week when you meet with the team members individually and as a group, create one new challenge that will result in a significant achievement that month. The easiest example is to break some company record that is relevant to your team, such as inventory issues, number of sales or customer service calls, fewer customer complaints, media placements . . . some measurable objective significant for your company. Uniting the team around these significant challenges creates at least a mental scoreboard to track achievement, though a real scoreboard works even better. Otherwise, it is like playing golf without keeping score, or poker without money: It might be fun for a short time but after a while, we lose focus and just start going through the motions.

But don't limit yourself to straight number challenges to make or break records. You can go anywhere with these challenges from small to large, such as:

- Challenge the finance team to spend a day in the field with the sales or service team.
- Challenge the sales team to spend two hours that day at the plant or in the warehouse.
- Challenge a manager to serve someone a cup of coffee.
- Challenge the engineering team to greet customers at the door.

If we make any of these things happen just 50 percent of the time, we will still achieve six milestones or team achievements per year. Once again, the key to any of the challenges, like any principle or process in this book, is that it must be genuine and maintained and not just something we say we did once. Coaches must always keep it going and "keep it real." If it is not, our intent will fade, so all we will have are empty actions that leave us back where we started, looking for something else to keep the team motivated.

If you are unsure about what might challenge and motivate your team, ask them. Turn to your top performers, and if they are not the most motivated, turn to the ones who are. Sometimes we have top performers who have good results despite the fact that they are not motivated, but that does not mean they are good team members or valuable overall to the team, as we learn in Chapter 7. First, we need people who are "motivatable." Given the chance to put an equally talented but more motivated person in place, a leader would, every time, get greater results from the team. If leaders have people on their teams who are not motivated by their jobs, they must take responsibility for it and help them find that motivation. If that doesn't work, they might decide to help those people find something they are motivated about and tell them to go do that for a living.

Get Your Team in "The New Guy/Girl Zone"

New employees are full of hopes and dreams. They look at every obstacle as an exciting challenge. They have grand dreams of success and no presuppositions about what can and cannot be done. Thus, the new guy often gets things done that cynics in the company would dismiss as impossible. Over time, however, two things usually happen to those new guys in management cultures: They leave when the challenge of their new jobs fade and opportunities aren't presented to them; or they become old guys, those cynics dwelling on the past and telling the new new guys why things can't get done. **This is what happens when the learning, energy, and challenges go away: Motivation disappears with them.**

That's why leaders like the plant executive must always ask, "Given the tools we have today, how do we achieve more?" When coaches challenge their teams to answer this question by achieving something greater than they have in the past, they will train and prepare for it and enter what I call The New Guy/Girl Zone.

Of course, it's a grind to keep this up. When you start out, it's like the beginning of a Little League baseball season. The grass is freshly cut. The excitement of playing the first games carries you. You have optimism. You watch things come together. Win or lose, it's fun. Everybody is excited despite the mistakes, and then you realize it is just game two. *Ten* more weeks of practice and games? But those ten weeks happen, no matter what. You can find a way to stay motivated and keep getting better or just keep losing.

In business and Little League, it is right to take the short-term pain of development for the long-term gain. The problem is, short-term pain can result in lost motivation that can be tough to recover. If a coach's bosses don't have confidence in the long-term plan and see *some* progress—if the players, especially your top performers, are losing their passion—there may be no long term. The consequences are the same: Lose too many games without the support of your team and any coach can get fired.

To keep the top of the team motivated when the grind starts, leaders tend to delegate key leadership tasks to their star players and top performers. We tell our superstars, now that they've developed these skills and are perceived as the team's top performers, we need them to lead the team, inspire them, and develop the team and take over drills. Delegating to them is an excellent motivational tool as long as we **delegate leadership on the field, not in coaching**. What that means is, top performers can be leaders of the team on the field, but they don't replace the coach. They run activities like scrimmaging and peer-to-peer presentations. In other words, delegating to top players can become part of a leader's motivational equation, but it cannot become the coaching equation. Baseball managers cannot have their shortstop coaching the team during a game plus playing shortstop, just as companies cannot have leaders responsible

> **Coaches let players lead players on the field, which is a step to making more coaches.**

for a team of sales reps plus their own sales quotas. A great short-stop can make perfect plays and get key hits, but he can't do that and be a great coach at the same time.

Create Leaders Motivated to Coach, Not Managers Motivated to Manage

Of course, this is what many companies do, create managers rather than coaches. When a company grows, it promotes its top performers to leadership positions, but it still expects them to do most of the work they were previously doing *and* take responsibility for the team. In most companies, this usually happens because we don't want to pay for a coach to lead the team in the first place and we fear losing the good work that the leader was responsible for. As a result, the newly minted leaders can't really delegate much, because the company has said, "I want you to be the creative director in charge of all of the other designers, but I still want you to do the designing you're doing." What exactly are they directing, then?

When companies do that, their leaders cannot coach. They can manage the team like leaders do in management cultures because that requires little involvement and accountability. They think, "I'm never getting fired for not being a manager, but I will get fired if I don't do my work. So if I just make my numbers, not blow anything up, and manage when I can, I'm safe." Trust me: Hire a leader to coach and that leader will not leave any project untouched, because they're responsible for all of them, especially if they have been coached by a leader in the past. But if leaders have to be responsible for their previous work too, that is highly demotivating.

Leaders in this situation are not growing their people; they are just maintaining operations. A company will get more done, get better results, and have a more motivated team if it has one leader managing three players and their projects, not four players with projects and one of them ostensibly managing them all.

Companies with leaders managing in these positions usually have a morale problem, which a coach must also take responsibility for. But in this case, words often speak louder than actions, because morale is the result of the team's feelings about what they are doing and the situation they are in, not of any actions leaders take.

To Change Does Not Always Mean to Get Better

Leaders who are coaches can and must mandate activities, but they can't expect change for the better immediately and that their teams will neatly fall into line in days or weeks or a month after years of what has been. That's why coaches need to give the teams some perspective. Coaches know that to change old feelings, they must first and foremost work hard to change and improve their teams' perspective—make them grateful and passionate for the opportunities they have. This is especially true if a company is not only adjusting to the cultural changes coaching brings but also going through downsizing or dealing with some difficult competitive issues, manufacturing issues, financial issues, etc. As my dad often told me, "Son, you think you have it bad, but trust me, someone out there has it a lot worse."

This is why so many leaders and companies spend millions every year to bring in tragedy speakers— motivational speakers who talk about facing and overcoming tragedies. Why does someone facing so

> Help the team see the blessings they have—the job itself, for one.

much tragedy make us feel good? Does that make us mean? Of course not! It is because the speakers ask us to change our perspective. A story of tragedy and overcoming it makes us grateful for what we have. They spark our emotions. We then look at our problems and realize that our issues are small. After the speech, everyone leaves determined to change their perspective and have a better outlook for pressing on and pursuing excellence. Then, the actions of motivation can take over to sustain that feeling.

Now, it doesn't necessarily take a motivational speaker or a story about triumph over immense tragedy to change our perspective. It does take a leader—a coach—to sit down with the team. In football, coaches give speeches before the game to mentally prepare the team. At halftime, they give a short speech either to get the team back on track or, if they are winning, to stay on track. Then, at the end of every game, regardless of the result, the coach gives a final speech recognizing the good and the bad of the game and setting the tone of what is to come.

Leaders can and must do the same thing in business to take responsibility for their team's morale—always thinking and speaking to them and preparing them for whatever part is coming next. They must see that the team morale is the sum of the individuals' morale. One individual with a bad attitude infects and diminishes everyone. And then the team is defeated. As their leader, do this: Acknowledge the hardships and hard feelings of a team member, but do not, under any circumstance, validate misery with sympathy. **The team isn't coming to us for sympathy. They are coming to us for perspective and direction. Sympathy is a valid and necessary emotion in life, but in this case, it's a toxin that only further poisons the well of bad morale.**

For example, an employee comes to you, the coach, expressing fear and sadness, anxious and depressed about conditions out of his control and negatively impacting his job. It might be the economy or something personal or the restructuring that's taking place. His leader, in an attempt to show sympathy, says something to the effect of "You [despondent employee] are right. Business is tough right now and there's nothing to be done about it but struggle on." Instead of feeling better, the employee is gloomier than ever. The leader acknowledged the feelings but also reflected and encouraged them. Word spreads, morale takes a dive, and the leader unintentionally hurts the team instead of helping. This is not to say that a leader of a team with bad morale is a bad person, but "Dumpster Morale" is often the result of a leader demonstrating sympathy instead of the empathy characteristic of great leaders.

Always think about and speak to your team the *right* way.

I first learned this when working with an executive at a Fortune 100 technology company as part of my coaching program there. Times were tough, and the latest round of layoffs at the company had just been reported. Morale in his office was down, and he asked me what he could do about it. I told him his team's morale had nothing to do with the company. Morale was down because of *him*. "What are you saying to them when they come to you?" I asked. He told me he said something like "I understand. All the layoffs are hard to watch. And it's tough competition out there. And the economy is brutal. We just need to work through this." Problem is, this executive wasn't empathizing with the team when he said these things (making the experience mutual and feeling what they were feeling). He was *sympathizing* with them (acknowledging their hardships). As a result, he wasn't holding them accountable for winning anymore and pushing them to do the very thing they probably

114 I NATHAN JAMAIL

needed to do to avoid being laid off themselves: Keep working harder. After working with him for months, he started to see my point and asked how to implement a change in direction and undo what he had said before. My advice was simple: Tell them the truth. I told him to say, "I've noticed morale is down, and I have found out that this is more my fault than your fault or anyone or anything's fault. I've allowed us to use excuses to have a pity party. I've sympathized with you instead of pushing you and myself to do more in spite of the obstacles and to work to overcome them." Now, when this executive tells his team to be grateful for what they have and keep working hard, their perspective starts to change, and morale starts to creep upward.

The executive learned that morale is not something you fix when it is broken, like the air conditioner in your home; it is something you must adjust, tweak, and maintain like the temperature of your home. The thermostat is your responsibility. You have to keep the temperature consistent, starting with your own attitude, and then give direction constantly, because morale is dependent on your direction as much as it is on perspective and gratitude. There may be uncertainty, resistance, confusion—words of defeat mixed with passion and desire—as you implement this playbook. Help your team through it. Guide them. Encourage them. Share your plan and the direction for *how* things will change. That's not only what will compel a team to share a leader's beliefs but also what will make the beliefs their own.

Takeaways:
Motivation and Morale

- The coach keeps the players motivated at all times and holds players accountable for motivating themselves and one another.

- Motivation is like food to our bodies! If we did not eat for three days, we would say we are hungry, not that food doesn't work. Motivation is the same; we must refill daily.
- Knowledge creates confidence, and when we are confident, we are more motivated.
- Motivated players with talent and skill will always outperform those without motivation.
- Morale is not about action, it is about feelings, and it requires a coach to direct the team members to change their perspective and feel gratitude when the feelings are bad.

Chapter 6
"BUILD YOUR BENCH": RECRUIT THE BEST PLAYERS

Getting better does not always come from hiring those with experience.

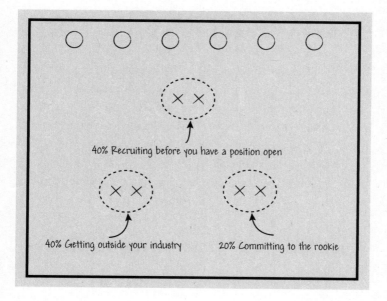

40% Recruiting before you have a position open

40% Getting outside your industry

20% Committing to the rookie

An engineering client of mine was having trouble with one of his company's leaders. This leader had a huge job with enormous responsibility that he was no longer doing very well. My client knew he needed a change. "Nathan," he said, "I've got to replace this guy, but I can't find enough engineering experience in this industry. There is no one out there with that experience."

"I get it," I said. "So why not go out and find someone with great skills and engineering experience outside the industry?" My client looked confused, so I explained, "Look for the attributes you want first, such as reliability, trustworthiness, drive, energy, positivity, and motivation to succeed. These things are harder to teach than industry specifics. Trust me, you can teach someone your business, but you can't teach someone to want to be successful. Let's find the best person and turn that person into the best in your industry."

"That will take at least three months to do," he said.

"That's fine," I told him. "It will be hard for those three months. Business may also be a little rocky during that time, but you're building something very powerful: the best player for the team that you need. In three months, you will start to see exponential growth year over year, because you have the right person."

My client wasn't initially sold, but that's because what I was saying flies in the face of conventional management hiring wisdom.

Hire the Right People, Not the Right Experience

The single biggest mistake most leaders make as managers is to look only for industry experience. Leaders see someone with industry experience and are willing to give up all the other things, such as focus and attitude. We dismiss things such as having a personal connection. We in effect say, "I like you. You have the passion and enthusiasm I need, but you don't have enough experience, so I'm going to go out and find a person with more experience whom I don't like very much because they'll hit the ground running." Typically, this method results in a bad hire, and when it does, we start making excuses as my client did that "all the good people are taken." But that's because we keep fishing in the same crappy industry pond. If other companies have fished out the whole pond, what is left? The fish other people threw back.

I'm not saying don't hire for skill set or avoid hiring for experience. I'm saying don't hire on industry experience alone. This is what I call a "fruits and roots" situation: Leaders are usually so focused on the fruits of the tree, we forget that it is the roots that grow the fruit. Experience counts too, but we need to remember that attributes and skills are the keys to success. Yes, industry experience can shorten a ramp-up period. Yes, the three-

> **The easiest way is not always right, even if it looks that way.**

month learning curve was difficult for my client to stomach in our instant gratification–based world—and really it can take up to six to twelve months in most situations. Yes, in theory, during the three to twelve months the person from outside the industry is learning the business, that person will underperform someone with experience and connections in the industry. **But if you go out of business because you backfilled that one position and needed to train the new person longer, you were going out of business anyway—no matter the short-term results someone with industry experience might have delivered.**

At the end of the day, a company needs revenue to survive but needs good people even more than revenue—because people make and grow revenue. This is why professional sports teams have rebuilding years. We can't all spend money like the New York Yankees and it doesn't always work even when we do. (And let's face it; the most recent Yankee dynasty was a core of home-grown players and role players that fit the team, not superstars.) In business, it is the same, only on a tighter timeline. We need to recruit for the best talent and fit, not just for experience. That's why we need to be constantly recruiting the talent and building our benches as coaches.

Build Your Bench: Find Talent before There Is a Need

Many of the leaders I work with get the bench-building concept wrong. Building the bench is not about filling open positions. It is about finding, meeting, and interviewing top talent before there's an open position. Remember: Coaches act before there is a problem. Professional sports teams have scouts all over the world looking for new talent. Can't you at least look around town?

I said and did the same thing for years until, one day, someone in HR asked me, "Why is industry experience important?" I started with my usual answers:

Filling open positions is not building the bench. It's hiring.

- Our industry is complicated and can have a long ramp-up period.
- I want a new employee to come in and hit the ground running.
- I want a person with industry contacts, able to connect with other leaders, to bring over some future clients, or possibly to add more talented team members to improve our team.
- And, honestly, it is easier on me.

So I told HR to keep industry experience as a requirement. But as I thought more about it, I started to see a different side of those reasons:

- Just because people understand an industry does not mean they are good at their jobs or are experts.
- Just because a person knows how to run does not mean he or she *will* run.
- Who is to say the relationships they have with other leaders and potential clients and employees are good ones (or that those people are even good employees)?
- Why is being selfish a legitimate excuse for not doing something better?

At the end of the day, how many times had I hired people, not to mention justified paying them a higher salary, because of their experience and contacts in the industry, and after all was said and done, none of that yielded anything of any value? More than I wanted to admit. This is how I, like most leaders, ended up hiring people with the bad attitudes I discussed in Part One. I assumed they possessed all the skills and experience I would later fear losing if they quit, because I had made industry experience such an important factor when I hired them. For me, I assumed these people had contacts that could become my team's customer base; for leaders in other divisions, it might result in connections to vendors and suppliers, politicians, government workers, technology and IT, trade associations, national and local businesses, or industry social networks. What I was really saying then was, the name of the company and the work my whole team did was not the source of those contacts—the individuals were. Meanwhile, while I had zeroed in on the benefits of industry experience, I had ignored concerns about how potential employees acted and made me feel in the interview. I ignored things such as the way they blamed others for all their struggles in their current positions, how everything was someone else's fault, or how their body language made me uncomfortable. Still, I thought I could change them. I reasoned that the environment they came from was bad, so with my cool, positive team, environment, and leadership, they would adapt. Not so.

From that moment on, I resolved that whenever I interviewed potential employees, I would avoid reviewing their résumés during the interview and instead focus on the *person* in front of me. I will discuss their previous work, but only with an eye toward assessing their skills. I don't talk about their responsibilities. I ask how they handled certain scenarios and discuss some "what if" situations. I then concentrate on how they answer, their energy, their attitude, and how I feel when they answer.

Think about it: What do we usually have the most of on our teams? Industry experience and company knowledge. So why continue to hire what we have the most of? Because most of us feel that our businesses or industries are too specialized or complicated to hire someone without experience. But I have worked with hundreds of companies over the past twenty years, across many industries, and I have learned one near-absolute truth: **Every company is complicated, different, and specialized, and therefore *they are all uniquely the same.***

Okay, every company is a little different and every industry has a learning curve. But as long as the work does not require a specific degree or license, coaches learn they can take a top performer from one industry to another and she or he will be great. So we can't hire someone to be a surgeon without a medical degree, but we can hire someone without hospital experience but with the skills to run something as complicated as the hospital the surgeons work in. I know I could take the best sales leaders at an established US product manufacturer and put them in sales in any industry, in any company, and in any economy, and they would become top performers in that industry. And I believe this is true in almost any department or job from finance to operations to design to editorial to construction to public relations and beyond. It even worked in engineering for the client I discussed at the start of this chapter—as soon as he saw past the company ego, that its industry was more difficult and specialized than others.

Coaches know that few people have jobs so complicated that someone with similar skills, but no knowledge of the industry, can't eventually do them. One of the best shot blockers of all time in the NBA, Dikembe Mutombo of the Congo, went to Georgetown on an academic scholarship. He also happened to be 7 feet 2 and athletic, so the Georgetown coach, John Thompson, recruited him to play center for the basketball team. He could teach Mutombo the game. Southwest Airlines hires teachers who have absolutely no airline experience because they are passionate about what they do and are used to handling cranky children in school, which is what we are like when our plane is delayed. They can teach them how to run the gate and aisle. I just hired a head bartender to run my office. I can teach her the computers and QuickBooks, but when she answers the phone? You can *feel* her.

What Makes Someone Great

I have several clients in the technology and engineering industries who often tell me I am wrong about all this. They tell me their company and industry is more advanced than other industries. Unfortunately, this view is just a bit of arrogance, self-defense, and pride used to validate their own self-worth. Here's what I mean by that. When I say to these clients, "If I have another client who makes concrete pipes, and they have an engineering position that pays five hundred thousand dollars a year, can you do it?" They'll tell me, "Heck, yeah." So just because they're engineers in a more "advanced" (meaning modern or high-tech) industry, they can learn another seemingly less advanced industry like concrete pipes. But an engineer from a concrete pipe company with the same skills and degree can't learn their industry?

Here is why leaders think this way: A lot of us have been doing something for such a long time in a certain industry that we gauge our worth by thinking, "I'm worth more money because I know this industry so well. I'm smarter because I've been doing it for fifteen years." Then they feel insulted when I tell them not to hire for industry experience; they think I am telling them that their experience is worthless. But I'm not insulting them. I just want them to look at it from the

> **Industry experience should not be how we gauge anyone's self-worth— including our own.**

other side: **What makes you great is not what you've been doing for fifteen years—what makes you great is you.**

The only one insulting anyone is you for hanging your hat on a job that you've been doing for fifteen years instead of the person that you are. Industry experience is not personal and thus doesn't replace personality. Look at it another way: How many times have our competitors hired one of our people and we are relieved because it was not one of our better people? Then, we go right out and look for the experience to replace that person who wasn't very good in the first place. We play a game of passing the "poor player" (many leaders have a less polite term, which I won't repeat here). In the end, how much is that industry experience really worth? I am not saying that all industry experience makes for poor candidates and that they are destined to be poor performers, nor am I saying we should never hire someone from our competitors. I'm just trying to hammer home once and for all that industry experience is often of less importance than other skills or experience, and we need to be able to let it go if necessary.

My engineering client did. They put aside their initial fear about the long learning curve and the assumption that engineers really need to know the products and features to make things. They hired a smart and driven engineer virtually right out of college. His learning curve would have been high anywhere. What my client soon realized is that without the industry experience, this guy was so great because he didn't have any of the "baggage" that comes with more experienced players. He did not know the history of what did and did not work. He didn't have any barriers to his own entry. He had the degree, but he also had the humility of the new guy and none of the arrogance. The new engineer simply did what he did best: He used his engineering skills to break down all the learning and is now one of the top engineers in the company.

A lighting manufacturer and distributor I worked with also let go of the chestnut that industry experience is essential. Three years ago, they hired a pharmaceutical rep to do their sales. After so many bad hires, my client decided to hire this rep, knowing his learning curve was going to be a little longer at the beginning but feeling great results would come from his skills long-term, with proper coaching. They taught him light switches, and in twelve months, he parlayed his sales skills onto the list of their top ten reps in the country. Sure, the first three months were rough. He had to learn the industry and build his base, and so from zero to 90 days, he was slower than everyone else. But from day 91 to 365, he was passing them all at rapid speeds. Today, he is their number one sales rep.

Commit the Most to Your Rookies

Of course, none of this works if leaders aren't willing to do the work required. If you build your bench and then hire the best person on that bench and you don't train them? That's your fault. What's not your fault is the occasional bad hire in spite of your efforts to recruit the right people. I know because there is no one who makes more bad hires than me. The difference between me and most is, as I said before, I hire fast and I fire faster. Say the person I hire, after ninety days, turns out not to be the right fit; if I get involved in my new hire's training, I will know within weeks if he or she is not a good fit, rather than years down the line. A bad hire, no matter the industry experience, will bring my entire team down. I need to find the person a different job in my organization or find them a job outside of my organization, and quickly.

In the NFL, rookies are tested, trained, prepared, coached, and tested again before they make the team. Rookies go through a tough training camp for several weeks and then preseason for a few weeks, until finally the decision is made to keep them on the team or release them. Coaches in business must show the same commitment

Don't sacrifice the important things for the easy things.

to our bench builders when we hire them (and really anyone new to our team and organization). We invest our time with the rookies so we can benefit from them in the future:

- Teach rookies everything you would want them to know, even if you think they already know it.
- Take the time to share written expectations.

- Be consistently and constantly available to them to help them understand the importance of their jobs.
- Create a training camp environment similar to professional sports, where playbooks and ideas are shared and tested.
- Have rookies shadow their leaders so they can understand how the leaders think and act.
- Have an industry learning session so the rookies know your version of the industry.

I have spent a lot of time inside company organizations and know that those who commit to the rookies are able to make better decisions about keeping or removing new hires.

In many cases when an organization does not have a leader involved in the boarding process, or what I refer to as the Training Camp, they end up keeping the wrong hire for too long.

So What Are You Waiting For? Make Talent a Priority

Being a coach in business is going to force your team to step up or step out, so start searching for talent before this happens. Don't get stuck thinking you need to keep those poor performers because you don't have anybody on the bench. A coach who always has another one or two top people identified to fill a position means talented people are always connected to you even if they are not on your team yet. Don't keep it a secret from your team either. If you don't, complacency will become less and less of an issue, I guarantee it.

Typically, the best people are the ones happy at their jobs already. Your job is to find them, and see if they would also be happy with you. If so, then convince them to join you. With today's social media and networking websites, there are many ways to achieve effective proactive recruiting. Depending on the position, the place to find talent will vary and might surprise you, but it won't come from the same industry mixers and events everyone else goes to. I recently met a driver from the largest independent hotel management company in the United States who was pure awesomeness; he had great energy, was very intelligent, and understood the real meaning of serving people. The leaders at this hotel management company were doing things right, because this driver loved his job even though he had had some much higher paying jobs in the past. He told me several times he loved coming to work. This type of person (positive, outgoing, motivated) will work in all organizations.

So here is your coaching homework: For six months, conduct one bench-building meeting or interview a week. Let prospective employees know what you are doing and why. This will also show future prospects that it is a difficult task to be a member of your team, and they will know, if an actual open position comes, to seize the opportunity. Let's break down the numbers: Even if you are successful only 10 percent of the time and take a few weeks off for vacation, this still gives you five new top-quality candidates!

The advice I give my kids is the same advice I give coaches: "No one is going to find you and give you something, so if you want something, you must go out and get it."

Yes, like all coaching skills, building the bench is a simple concept but difficult to find the time to execute and sustain. Reminds me of my aim to go to the gym and work out. Schedule it, mandate it, and make it happen.

Takeaways:
Building the Bench

- Identify talent before you need them so you get what you want and not what you will settle for.
- Hire the enthusiasm and skill, and teach the industry knowledge—stop shooting for hitting-the-ground-running and start focusing on practicing with passion.
- Recruit and interview as a weekly task: Good employees are hard to find.
- Commit and invest time in the new hires immediately.

Chapter 7
MAKE TOUGH DECISIONS

If you've got someone not doing the job, on any level and with any time served, you need to coach them up or remove them from the position.

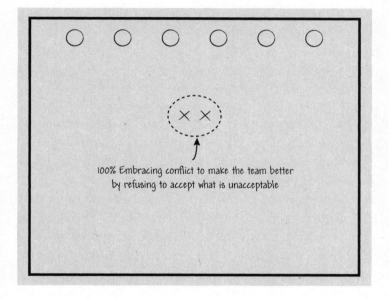

100% Embracing conflict to make the team better
by refusing to accept what is unacceptable

"**S**ell your winners and take the gains; ride your losers and see if they can recover so you don't take a loss." I hear this philosophy about buying and selling stocks all the time. And I think it is almost always the exact opposite of what we should do, not only with money but also as business leaders: Keep your winners, they are *winners*; dump your losers, they are *losers*. Of course, underperforming players in business (and sports) can improve with a change in direction (coaching) or a change of team or scenery. That's *if* we can make the necessary changes.

My football coach was not always the nicest guy, but he was always up-front, honest, and clear. These attributes are what mattered to us as players, not how nice he was, and we played hard for him. We knew where we stood. He mandated that we have a positive attitude or leave the team, and he made sure we were ready to play *every day*. If a star player was a slacker or was making his teammates miserable, the coach directly addressed him, and if the player refused to comply, he found the bench and then the bleachers. The coach didn't do what all too many leaders do in business: Reward the bad behavior by giving the player more responsibility, thus allowing the bad attitude to infect more players. He didn't isolate the player from the team so he would affect only himself; a team player is never alone, so it won't work. He met the problem head-on. He *coached*.

Not that saying this makes tough decisions any easier for a coach. If you have ever seen the HBO series *Hard Knocks*, which follows an NFL team through their training camp, you know what I am talking about. One of the hardest parts to watch is when the coach calls players into his office to let them know they are not going to make the team. He does it with a heavy heart; he knows he is telling the players their dreams of playing in the NFL will not happen, at least not now. It's never easy for the coach to say this, but it is necessary—and what's more, he knows he'll need to do it next year too if he is successful and remains the coach.

Coaches in the NFL know they must make changes to the teams quickly and as needed to ensure a win for everyone, or their jobs are on the line. Not so in business. Coaches may know part of building a winning team is to get rid of all nonwinning players, but here are the biggest reasons we've covered for not making the tough decision to move them out:

- We are selfish and are worried about the time and resources it would take.
- We avoid conflict and prefer to be nice to our people, giving them every chance and benefit of the doubt.
- We confuse player tenure with player loyalty.
- We fear lost business owing to losing the body and not having a replacement on the bench.

Following our five essential coaching principles and the actions of Chapter 6, all these reasons can now be remedied. But too many leaders, even after building their benches, still wait for attrition rather than make places on the team now. We may talk to our employees about having to make tough decisions, but we avoid those tough decisions ourselves when it comes to the team, choosing not to coach our nonwinners up or out, and hoping against hope that the situation gets better or at least no worse. But bottom to top, a bad situation rarely does get better and usually gets worse without action.

This is especially true when it comes to the people who are fun to have around but whose work is just "meh." Let's say someone has been working for you for a couple of years and that person does an okay job—not making you famous but not killing you either, a bit of a slacker but most everyone really likes him or her. Too many leaders accept that person's mediocre work instead of remembering that this is still a bad body regardless of the likability. Leaders must know that if they don't hold that person accountable, their top performers will say, "If the boss just lets that slacker sit there, why should *I* work so hard?" Now everybody on the team comes down to the bad body's level. Everything is questioned, including their leadership. Then, the top performers who refuse to go down to that level quit and become appreciated somewhere else. But guess who never quits. The mediocre slacker.

But slackers are not the toughest people to deal with when a leader needs to build a winning team. What about the long-timers who are stuck in their ways and have grown complacent, as we discussed in Part One? What about the Life-Suckers who deliver results but whose attitudes bring the rest of the team down? What about the really good guys whom everyone likes but who are just in the wrong job? **Those are three kinds of underperformers we're likely to encounter in our businesses: Complacent Long-Timers, Life-Suckers, and Good Guys.** To understand these three types is the first step in the coach's job of making that tough decision to move them up or move them out—or suffer the consequences.

The Complacent Long-Timer

I was conducting an initial interview with a client in the energy industry to decide if I would be a good fit to work with the company. The leaders below the CEO had read my previous books, implemented some of the programs, and called to ask if I would be willing to conduct some training and executive coaching for the leadership and their CEO. But in my initial interview, only the leadership team was in the room. They were excited about the potential of coaching, but when I asked what the CEO thought of the idea, they all looked at one another and said, "Well, we thought you could meet with him and find out. We don't think he is going to agree with us one hundred percent . . . but he *needs* to."

Despite my apprehension about this approach, I agreed to the meeting, and we discussed the principles of my coaching program. The CEO agreed with most of the ideas but one: the need for accountability by his underperforming employees. Turned out, this CEO *knew* he had underperformers on his team, especially employees who had been with him a long time and now, he felt, gave him minimum performance. So I asked him why he accepted it. He said, "Because they have been loyal to me for over twenty years."

"No disrespect," I said, "but loyalty is not shown in years of employment. You paid them for those years. The reason they stayed and continue to stay is because you paid them. I'm not saying that they don't care, or things have not been great for many of those years. But loyalty is shown through continued contribution, not through tenure."

The CEO seemed to agree, so I asked him, "Do you have a plan to address your concerns about the performance they are giving you?"

"I have many times and will continue to address the issue," he replied. "But they are not going to change."

"Then it sounds like they need to find a new job outside the organization," I said.

He did not agree with me . . . and I mean at *all*. "Absolutely not," he said. "These guys are untouchable and will be here as long as they want."

Of course, this CEO's employees were untouchable only because the CEO refused to do anything about them. At that point, we both knew this would not be a good fit for either of us. I wasn't taking anything *from* him or the team, or disparaging the past success of these longtime employees. I simply believed the business could be a lot *more* successful if the company followed my coaching principles and actually dealt with the underperforming people. So I thanked him for his time and told him that I had truly enjoyed our meeting and I was impressed with his success, but that my program would not work in an organization that will not hold all members accountable for the job that needs to be done.

Turns out, this incredibly successful CEO was no different from most leaders in dealing with the Complacent Long-Timers. Complacent Long-Timers are employees who have been at a company for a long time and lost passion for the job and thus no longer deliver the results they used to. The reasons for the loss of passion and resulting complacency vary from boredom to laziness. Maybe the humdrum of routines and tasks, methodically repeated year after year after year, have tired them out and left them depressed and working only for a paycheck. Maybe they desire a change and a challenge but fear taking the risks associated with looking for additional or new work.

Stop confusing tenure with loyalty: We don't owe people anything for just showing up.

Whatever the reason, Complacent Long-Timers cause everyone to suffer, especially when they are leaders in the organization and have the sway of seniority. If other, less-tenured employees take the complacency of the long-timer as an example of how to act in the company, the complacency will only grow. It will spread like weeds and over years—yes, years!—those substandard results will become ingrained in the day-to-day culture of the company.

By the time the leadership is no longer willing to accept the Complacent Long-Timers' behavior, leaders of those companies have an even bigger problem: Performances have declined and the loss to the company—whether actual losses or less success than could have been realized—has become huge. If leaders want the employees to change, and the employees want to change, the task is now enormous. They have to overcome a huge delta of underperformance: a stagnant mess where the employees *and* the business and relationships they're responsible for are stuck, in decline, or have disappeared entirely. To restore flow, the employees need to hustle like rookies, finding and building new relationships and business and work as hard as ever to overcome the perception of mediocrity. Usually, their egos can't handle that, and they lack the confidence to do so. In most cases, the employees are not willing to do the work and end up leaving (of their own volition or because they're fired). At the end of the day, everyone loses. The employee, the team, and the company each have to start over. **All because of the leader's inability to make a tough decision about a Complacent Long-Timer.**

That's what seemed to be happening with the energy company I met with. The company is still successful, but the CEO's status quo still rules. When I spoke to my contact on the leadership team a year later, he said they were in the same spot as before: Owing to the CEO's inability to hold everyone accountable, the good employees were frustrated and looking to leave. An entire culture of unhappiness was being fostered, and unless something drastic changed, the CEO would continue to accept complacency. Why wait for that? We don't owe anyone a job; we just owe them the opportunity to earn and keep their job. Let me be perfectly clear: I worked for Sprint for more than nine years, and I gave them everything I had for those years. But they paid me very well and I loved my job. They owed me *nothing* for just showing up. We must expect our employees to show up and want to play every day. Like professional athletes who no longer have the ability or desire to play for their teams and compete at the highest level, Complacent Long-Timers can no longer be on your team.

A coach who stops putting the best players on the field stops getting paid for being a coach or, if no one is holding that coach accountable, loses the confidence of the team. Think about it this way: Most athletes compete for their jobs every year. If employees had to interview for their jobs every year, most wouldn't get rehired. Ask most leaders how many of their employees they would still hire, knowing what they know today, and they'll say fewer than half. My message to those leaders is this: Do those Complacent Long-Timers know it? If they don't, that's our fault! Those employees don't know we want to fire them for being bad. They may not even know what they're doing wrong.

Complacent Long-Timers are not without hope for a turn-around, but leaders really have to push them, and they really have to respond to improve their attitude, find their passion, and work their hardest. We are doing no one any good keeping them around. A win-win could be to move them to another team or company. In sports and business, it used to be that the best players started and finished their careers with the same teams. It was expected that they do so. Today, few people get the proverbial gold watch, and professional sports are filled with stories of players who are traded for the good of the team and the player. The Complacent Long-Timers end up thriving on the new team, and the old team then has room to turn to its bench and bring in someone—maybe someone else who needs that change, maybe a rookie ready to move up—who will deliver the results the team needs.

> **An employee's getting complacent is his or her choice. Allowing that employee to remain complacent is the coach's choice.**

The Life-Sucker

The Life-Sucker is the easiest to spot of the three types we're covering here but not the easiest to handle. Life-Suckers are not team players, do not follow direction, and just, well, suck the life out of a team. Unfortunately, unlike the Complacent Long-Timer, Life-Suckers sometimes have impressive knowledge and deliver great results. As a result, Life-Suckers can grow very powerful. Leaders are thus hesitant to deal with the Life-Sucker because it can mean a real loss of business. But remember: Everything about a Life-Sucker is powerful. Attitudes are infectious, and a bad attitude makes for bad business. A powerfully bad attitude is like the blare of a trumpet.

So what's a coach to do? I had a Life-Sucker like this in my company who was not only a great performer—she was my superstar. But she was always bringing the team down.

This happened most noticeably in team meetings. I would propose a change in direction or a logical goal like increasing our revenue share from 15 to 75 percent, and her immediate response was "That can't be done" or "We can't do that and here's why" or "We have never done that." This was one of my top people. The team viewed her as an unofficial second in command. So, when she said those things, everyone listened and thought, "Well, if she said so, then it has to be true." Problem was, she didn't *really* think that. Two hours later, she would call me and say, "Okay, so I got this figured out and here is what we are going to do. . . ." She would come up with her own solution for how we were going to head in a direction as a company or a group. But what good was that for the actual group and the six other managers who left

> It is impossible to be a *great* employee and have a bad attitude.

the meeting thinking something couldn't be done, and still thought so?

Understand, this person was not waving her own flag; she was waving our team's flag, but no one saw that. She left with an agenda in her head and came up with a solution the others couldn't see. Instead, what the team saw was a naysayer who contradicted my coaching vision and then came up with a plan in isolation from the team. I needed her either to wave the team's flag in front of the team or to get off the team. I needed her to be saying in front of the team all the things she was saying to me one-on-one. I needed people to see her as a leader of the team's agenda and not her own agenda, or I needed her to take that agenda somewhere else. Which is exactly what I told her in a documented meeting.

Because this person had become so powerful with her performance, I couldn't fight her. So I didn't. I empowered her. I explained what I saw happening and how much power she had: "When you leave the meeting and then you go and fix the problem, every other manager thinks that because you said it can't be done, they can't do it either. It doesn't matter if you solve it later. You're making my job a lot harder by creating doubt where it doesn't need to be. Now, I can't fight you and I don't want to. I want you on this team. I need you to be a leader and that means being a part of this team and supporting this team by lining up with them, or you may need to go find joy in a different job."

The good news for me was, she lined up. She wanted to be a leader and loved hearing that the team and I saw her as a leader. She had no idea she was creating problems for the team. In her mind, she was just laying out what the obstacles to success were. She thought everybody else was leaving the meeting and going through the same process she was, not that she had her own process and everyone else was stuck on what she said in the meetings.

Unlike the Snowman, the Life-Sucker we met in Chapter 4, this person did not think she was doing the people on the team a favor by being a "realist" in meetings. She actually was a top performer, while the Snowman blamed everyone else for why he wasn't succeeding more. She now knew that she had the power to change and control the situation. She also knew I would fire her before I promoted her if she did not change. The good news is, she changed, and became one of my best employees—not to mention started to love her job, not just improve her performance, again. That said, I had similar conversations with the Snowman and employees like him and, unfortunately, they did not or could not change, so I helped them to find opportunity elsewhere. The important part is to have the conversations.

But this is a huge jump. Before we can even have the conversation about how to remove Life-Suckers from the team, we should ask ourselves what we have done as the leader to make them aware of their issues and, more important, make them aware of the impact they have on the team. In many cases, like my top performer, Life-Suckers are not aware that they are Life-Suckers, or they don't realize the negative impact they have on the team. It's easy to blame them before we blame ourselves. And yes, we should be sensitive to situations outside the office that might be affecting the Life-Sucker. But even if the struggles are the result of personal or psychological and not professional problems, we cannot be hesitant in our approach. By all means be sensitive and conscious of deeper problems, but Life-Suckers have brought their problems to our teams and made their problems everyone's problems. Fellow team members and customers/clients are also feeling it and find it difficult to breathe when the air gets sucked out of the room.

During my workshops, I ask leaders, "If someone stole one thousand dollars from the company, would you fire them?"

Without fail, everyone says, "YES!" The scary fact is, Life-Suckers with negative attitudes will cost at least ten times that much money over and over again. In business, just as in life, we are judged by our actions, not by our words. Leaders must believe that having a great attitude is important and then mandate it. We're not being nice to the Life-Suckers when we don't do this; we're being mean to those who aren't Life-Suckers.

There are right and wrong ways to approach these employees, but leaders must not be selfish and scared. We *must* make Life-Suckers aware of their attitudes, give them an opportunity to change, and make the change ourselves if they refuse in word and then in deed. **Remember: You can practice what to say and do if you discover a Life-Sucker has personal problems. You can work on being understanding, but there is no excuse for letting the behavior just go on.**

The Good Guy

Leaders often think of their bad employees and hires as bad people. They think about the people who lied about their skills and experience to get the job, who were abusive to their teams and the staff, who simply up and quit when a better offer came along, who committed a crime. . . . And don't get me wrong. These people *are* bad (or at least their actions are). But not all bad employees are bad people. Many times, they are the *nicest* people in the world but a bad fit for a particular job. Bad hires can be Good Guys and have all the positive energy, commitment, and passion in the world, but we didn't find out they lacked the skills and attributes needed for the job until they "took the field."

This is why the Good Guy is the hardest of the tough decisions to deal with, emotionally. To paraphrase Sally Field at the

Oscars, we like them, we *really* like them. Good Guys do lots of things right, give us everything they have, and truly are doing their best. Unfortunately, it is not good enough. But whether it is a lack of skills or the wrong job to begin with, they can't move up. Whatever the reason, they are Good Guys but bad employees.

As we discussed in Chapter 6, I'm not talking about hiring someone just because he or she is a Good Guy and *ignoring* the missing skills and attributes. I'm a likable guy who loves football, but I would be a bad draft pick for the Houston Texans football team even if I gave every game my all. They would be foolish to waste a roster spot on me. Truth is, we like to believe and do believe—and tell our children—that you can do anything you want to do in life. **But that does not mean you are going to be good at it or that, if you devote all your time and energy to it, you'll develop the skills and confidence to do it.**

Good Guys come to us in many ways. Sometimes we are desperate enough to look past the résumé to focus only on the people we like. Sometimes we promote someone we really like but whose new responsibilities lie outside their current field of expertise. No matter the reason, when Good Guys go bad, it is usually obvious to everyone, including the Good Guys. They may try harder, work later, and give it their all, but at the end of the day, they go home disappointed or frustrated, in many cases feeling bad not just about their job but about themselves. As leaders, we don't want to hurt their feelings, so we keep encouraging them long after the expiration date and tell them to keep trying, but this leads to our being frustrated, the team struggling, and the Good Guy feeling shame, embarrassment, and guilt.

> **Not everyone is equal in every way.**

Dealing with Good Guys is hardest when they are not new employees but longtime employees who are not complacent but simply stuck. I have a client with a great team of leaders and they all, for the most part, care about their jobs, their teams, and the company. One of these leaders is one of the nicest and most genuine guys I have had the opportunity to work with in my career. Mr. Good Guy, Mr. G for short, has been with the company for more than ten years and in the industry for thirty years. He had great knowledge and experience and his efforts were just as great. However, there was a problem: No matter how many hours he worked, or how hard he tried, he could not grasp the concept of leading a sales team . . . and he was the *VP of sales*!

Mr. G understood the sales process and the operations of the business, but he could not grasp team development. Mr. G would probably not admit this to anyone, but I knew he knew it. Drive, desire to do the job, and pride kept him going, but it was not enough. Now, you might be thinking, "Nathan, didn't you say earlier that desire, drive, passion, and ambition are essential attributes?" The answer is "Yes, I did. But these have to be directed toward the right things." Mr. G does have the passion for the job, but his passion is not enough. No matter how hard he tries, he cannot do the job. No amount of effort or care will get Mr. G to the top because he is in the wrong job. And it would be my client's failure if they did not address the problem and continued to let Mr. G struggle, by not making the tough decision to confront him.

It wasn't that Mr. G wasn't good at the game; he was like a lineman being asked to play quarterback. I told my client, Mr. G's boss, "You are doing him an injustice by allowing him to stay in his role and go on struggling, and if you don't move him sooner rather than later, you will ruin him and in turn lose a great contributor to the team. By placing him in a better fit, like

VP of operations, he would skyrocket to stardom! He would be happier in the end and more successful, and the organization would benefit."

My client agreed, in theory, but still couldn't bring himself to confront Mr. G and make the change. If he had, he might have learned what I have after years of coaching: **The Good Guy's underperformance may be difficult to confront, but the results can be some of the most rewarding tough decisions in the long run.** After all, someone has to help a person like Mr. G to get out of his situation, even if it means offering less money or a demotion, and that person is his leader. Leaders like my client do Good Guys no favors by keeping them in a job in which they're miserable and feel altogether inadequate. Most times, even with the demotion or reduction in pay, they are happier than doing something they really can't do well.

Many times in my career, I have had employees like Mr. G—employees who, after I became their manager, had to sit down with me to discuss their placement. At these meetings, they were mad and upset with me—one even called me a monster—but always, each time (sometimes days, maybe months later) they called or e-mailed and said they were happier. Maybe part of it was because they no longer worked for me—Good Guys can clash with good coaches—but I believe it is because they were now doing something they could be successful doing.

Have the right people doing the right things at the right time.

Having the ability, discipline, courage, and commitment to help our people be better, even when it means making tough decisions, is what leads to success. Stop assessing the problems but not making the changes. Make the tough decisions about these types of employees—and anyone else who brings the team down or holds them back from being the best they can be—and everyone will benefit.

Takeaways:
Make Tough Decisions

- It is never the right decision to keep a person who is not the best fit in the job.
- Once you know a person is not a good fit for a job, your job as a leader is not to be selfish and avoid conflict but to make a move.
- Remember: All great long-term rewards require short-term work and pain.
- Complacency can kill results, morale, and success faster than the competition in any industry or market.
- If someone has a bad attitude, it is their fault, but if you pay them, it is your fault!

Chapter 8
TREAT THE VICTIM DISEASE

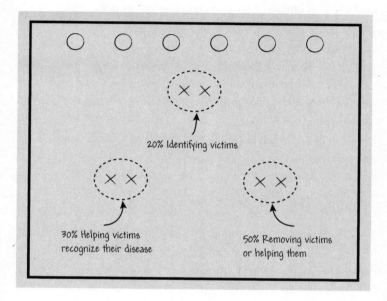

In the 1993 movie *Addams Family Values*, Pugsley and Wednesday are sent to a summer camp, where Wednesday battles constantly with the prim, privileged, and protected Amanda. At the lakefront, the overeager counselor, Gary, prepares the campers to learn about lifesaving and makes Wednesday and Amanda "buddies."

"Now, one of you will be the drowning victim and the other one gets to be our lifesaver," Gary says.

"I'll be the victim!" Amanda shouts proudly.

"All your life," Wednesday replies.

A lot of leaders, including myself, could have used Wednesday's expertise in identifying who plays the victim for our businesses. After all, Wednesday Addams was right about Amanda and right on a deeper level too. The problem is that we live in a society that tends to *raise* victims. We don't teach our kids to fail; we think everyone deserves to win and get a medal. We don't accept that any problem might be because of *us*. When children think teachers hate them, most parents go in and complain about the teacher. It can't be the kid. Somebody is *causing* our children to act this way. Blame it on the teacher, the school, the curriculum, the school lunch . . . but not little Suzie and little Johnny. Now little Suzie and little Johnny have résumés, and chances are, one of them is working for us.

Identifying the Victim Disease

In business, the single most defining symptom of victim disease is a rapid, never-ending stream of excuses. Those most severely infected never run out of people or things to blame, making any lack of success beyond their control. Victims justify their performance or lack of performance by blaming the lack of opportunities. In their warped world, everything is an attack upon them. When challenged on this point, victims typically respond the way they do to most feedback, criticism, and coaching—by going into defensive lockdown. All this, if not recognized, addressed, and removed, will become the greatest enemy of a team's winning attitude. Victims can affect results and morale as much as any underperformer. Yet they thrive in businesses because leaders allow them to be victims and have no desire to hold them accountable for their "victiming."

A lot of people behave like victims because we allow them to be victims.

Problem is, we're not dealing just with the victims we already have; we're hiring them to work for us. We could have avoided hiring many of those infected with victim disease in the first place, but most leaders don't do the work to identify obvious victims during the hiring process. Sometimes, this is because those leaders are victims themselves, and we like people who are like us. It's not that these leaders are acting maliciously; they are acting sympathetically, which is one of the reasons sympathy is not a characteristic of a strong leader. When someone says I couldn't do this or achieve that, the leader thinks, *I had the same problem. This person never had a chance. I will give him a chance.* More often, though, we fail to spot victims in the hiring process by failing to ask questions that offer a prospective hire a chance to make excuses and blame someone or something for why they have not achieved anything.

The easiest thing to listen for in interviews are answers to questions that find out, right or wrong, if a person can or will blame other people or things outside of their control of any situation. A simple question like "Have you ever been part of a project that failed but it wasn't your fault?" will fast let me know if I have a potential victim in front of me. A victim will answer something like "I did my part, but the [editorial, marketing, engineering, art, etc.] department didn't get their piece [in, right, approved, etc]." The answer may be true, but how the person answers it and my follow-up questions tell me as much about that person as what he or she said: Is he or she defensive? Angry? Resentful? Taking any responsibility?

Here are some other questions that can lead to a round of the blame game:

- If people have already left their previous employer, ask them why *and* then follow up with

"Can you go back?" and "Would they hire you back?"—listen for how much they point a finger at someone or something else for any reasons why not.

- Ask them to describe their favorite boss and their least favorite boss and listen to how they describe them—do they naturally just start blaming the least favorite boss for their problems?
- Ask them to talk about good and bad relationships they had at work—listen for where they take responsibility and abdicate it.

Simply put, victims do not take responsibility for their actions or failures. I remember interviewing a person for a manager's position who mentioned how his current boss "did not let me be successful, but if I could only do things my way, I would be more successful." He told me about situations that failed because of others, but he couldn't name any failure of his own. By asking the candidate how or why this was true, I might have seen the flashing sign over his head, screaming VICTIM. But I was blind, and he had the résumé, and the answers I was looking for, and he seemed likable enough, so I hired him.

Only later, with the coaching and help of my boss, did I start to see the characteristics of his victim disease and realize the negative effects they had on our business and our leadership team. If I had done a better job of recognizing his victim disease and avoiding it, I would have done a better job for my team. I understood that I could not go back and change the past, so as a leader, it was now my job to treat the victim.

Recognizing and Dealing with Victims

So how do we recognize a person with victim disease already in our business? It can be difficult to recognize when someone is acting like a victim because one thing victims will not do is call themselves victims. In many cases, they do not see themselves that way. I say this as someone who has regrettably hired his fair share of victims, missing the signs, which I did not recognize at the time.

Leaders in the position of dealing with victims in their businesses, remember the coaching principles: Embrace the conflict and face the problem. Confronting victims brings conflict and a lot of it, but this is the only way to help the person and the team. Be prepared. Practice your meeting with a peer or mentor prior to the meeting. Help the victim understand why you see him or her as a victim and, most important, that being a victim is costing him as an individual and is affecting the team and the organization. Help the victim understand that being a victim is a choice, and not being a victim is a choice as well.

As leaders, it is our job to:

1. Identify victims.
2. Help them recognize their beliefs and behaviors.
3. Help them go from victims to victors or go someplace else.

Recently, the owner of the fitness club where I work out brought me in to help him coach his team of personal trainers. His concern was how these trainers were communicating with his customers. He wanted the trainers to understand how what they say and do not only reflects on them but also on the business as a whole. Any trainer and gym can get results, but good communication would differentiate him from his competitors, build relationships, and generate great word-of-mouth.

As I started talking to and working out with the trainers, I zeroed in on one trainer immediately. He was an athlete with a real chip on his shoulder. Now, I am not an athlete nor do I have much experience with weight lifting. This trainer, who I would see a couple of times a week, became extremely impatient with me because I couldn't remember what a power clean, one of the moves, looked like from one session to the next. But it wasn't just me; he seemed to rub everyone the wrong way. He yelled at the part-time staff to clean up quicker. He yelled at a friend of mine as she worked out because he felt she was not taking her workout seriously, and he made her feel stupid.

I tell every client I work with what I tell myself: It is our job to make people feel special. That's not just for salespeople, the hospitality industry, or customer service. Maybe you have a product that makes someone feel special or use words that make someone feel special when they walk into your office or department. Whatever it is, the best people make other people feel special. This trainer seemed not to know that rule and had forgotten he was there to serve us.

Victims never make anyone feel special, except those who enable them.

So I pulled him aside and asked him why he was so angry with me and why he thought people like me were even there. He immediately got defensive and even seemed offended by my questions. "People like you don't listen," he said, "because they don't want to get better. They just want to come in and play." He

TREAT THE VICTIM DISEASE

was frustrated that he takes his job so seriously while everyone else comes in just "to play." He didn't care that I, like most of his clients, had busy lives and came to him to escape—that his life might be wrapped around weight lifting and training, but for his clients, it was a one-hour task in the day. He thought we weren't serious about it, didn't love it, or didn't care about it. That didn't mean it wasn't a priority for us. I tried to explain all of this and more to him—to show him he was missing the point, that we found value in this escape to the gym and he needed to make us feel special during that time. I wanted him to see it was like owning a bar. We go to a bar to escape our worries; when you own the bar, it *is* your worry.

As I pressed him further and asked why he thought it was acceptable to yell, the excuses started about why he was the way he was. His bosses? "They renewed my contract, but they won't let me do what I want to do." It went on and on with lines like that. It was all about poor little him. One day, I showed up and he was sitting over in a corner pouting. When I asked him why, he said, "Well, I wasn't supposed to come in today." I told him they were paying him and if they wanted him to stand on his head and spin like a top, then he should spin like a top. His job was to make a difference for the people who pay the gym and for the bosses who pay him. And that led to an entirely new conversation full of excuses regarding his childhood and college woes.

Unfortunately, this trainer had a terminal case of victim disease and eventually, after ninety days, my client fired the guy. A couple of weeks later, someone told me they had lunch with him and they told me he said, "Well, they *wanted* me to be fired." He said they put him in situations where he would lose his temper so they could fire him. Everything from what he was required to do, to his attendance, to what he got paid—someone did something wrong to put him in that spot. Unfortunately, he'll probably play the victim the rest of his life.

Change the Victim to Victor or Change the Player

At Sprint, my teams supported companies, such as Radio-Shack and Best Buy, that sold our products and services. Once, when I took over a new market, one of the existing sales managers told me the reason the team was struggling: "We can't sell our product out there because it doesn't work well enough." How was this person a victim? On the face of it, this certainly sounded as if the team had legitimate reason for failing to build its business. It was true that we launched a product with network coverage inferior to that of some of our competitors . . . *three years before.* In the three years since, our coverage and products had gotten significantly better and worked as well as anyone else's in the market. By maintaining the excuse that our products didn't work well enough, this sales manager could rationalize any lack of success.

I hear similar complaints from leaders and teams in every industry: My product or service just isn't competitive with the other products out there. Victims accept this as fact and thus an insurmountable obstacle. But as happened at Sprint, facts can change, and sometimes those obstacles aren't insurmountable at all. Look at the top performers on the same team as the victim: Are they struggling too? Are they focusing on how bad things are or working hard to overcome them? What really did not work well enough at Sprint was my sales manager. Obstacles in life and business are facts; bad things happen and people do bad things. But being a victim in response to those obstacles or actions is a *choice.* We all face obstacles, but victims don't know the difference between an obstacle and an excuse.

Obstacle—Excuse—Solution

- **An obstacle is a fact:** a problem we must (and CAN) overcome (competition, industry issues, economy, market trends)
- **An excuse is a result:** a reason we did not overcome the obstacle to achieve our goal—why we lost or are losing "the game"
- **A solution is a result:** how we overcame the obstacle to win or push forward on achieving our goals

Because of his performance and because he still felt it was not his fault and that the company was the one to blame for his failure, I encouraged my sales manager to go out and have a fresh start. I told him that this team was not a good fit for him and he was probably right that the company and I had failed him—but not for the reason he thought. I had failed him because I was unable to help him treat his victim disease. That's because I do not believe victim disease is terminal and all victims are worthless to a company. I believe people can change their beliefs and behaviors if they decide to do so. Leaders should help victims see the power that no longer blaming other people or circumstances can give them, and how it makes them better people.

Leaders must help those who make the choice to be a victim to make better choices, or we have to help them move outside the team or company. That's *our* choice. It is not enough to help victims fight their disease; leaders must continue to coach them, because the disease can return. As coaches and leaders, we cannot change those who do not want to change, so we must be able to recognize the signs of a refusal to change and remove those victims from the organization.

If my client's trainer and my sales manager had listened to what we were saying and recognized their problems, we could

Winning is not about skill—it's about mind-set.

have worked with them. But they both accepted no responsibility or accountability. They kept blaming everyone and everything and in no way said, "Help me get better" or "Let me know when I'm doing something wrong." Victims who do that open themselves up to further coaching activities, such as scrimmaging. That's how victims become victors. They do what I tell my kids all the time: "Don't give any person or thing power to determine your success." We control everything we do and how we do it. Leaders must help victims understand that accepting responsibility does not mean weakness—it means strength.

Takeaways:
Treating the Victim Disease

- Like so much in coaching, the easy part is identifying this problem; the hard part is addressing it and fixing it.
- Most victims do not know they are victims or don't see themselves as victims.
- Recognize the disease and make people aware they have it, then remove the victim disease from the person or remove the person from the team.

- Know that leaders who are victims can create more victims because they sympathize with them and they enable them to remain victims.
- Look for the blame game when interviewing prospective new hires.

Chapter 9

AVOID THE BIGGEST MANAGEMENT TRAPS

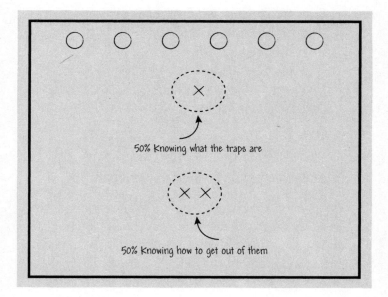

50% Knowing what the traps are

50% Knowing how to get out of them

Despite all I know about turning managers into coaches and striving to be a coach myself, I still fall into management traps that keep great leaders and managers from being great coaches. I know what the traps are and even see them coming sometimes, but I have to work hard to avoid them. And unless we make conscious efforts to avoid these traps or have an exit strategy when we don't, we will stay snared and struggle in them and eventually give up on some, if not all, of the coaching skills and principles we have worked on so far. So, before I let you go from the activities and actions of coaching to the culture of coaching, I want to cover the five biggest management traps coaches fall into.

The Five Biggest Management Traps

1. Trap #1: Coaching is difficult and redundant.
2. Trap #2: My team is already great.
3. Trap #3: Checking the box
4. Trap #4: Allowing bottom performers to leave on their own timeline
5. Trap #5: Not believing

Trap #1: Coaching Is Difficult and Redundant

Coaching is a time-consuming and often repetitive activity. We love to say, "Focus on the basics," but it takes constant effort for our actions to match these words. The trap is rationalizing the time and difficulty of sustaining a culture when we say, "I don't have the time to coach anymore," and that excuse's ugly stepsisters "Our people already know this stuff" and "We have already practiced this topic." To stay on course and stay out of this trap, remind yourself and your team that **although we have already worked on skills or disciplines and know and have improved them, we cannot stop practicing them.** A professional baseball player will practice catching grounders and pop flies from tee ball until he retires. He never believes he's perfect. The practice is rarely new and exciting, but the desire to become a *better professional* and keep getting better is. The same is true in business: If we keep focusing on being better at everything we do, then our business will get better.

Sure, it's easier to start than sustain. Often leaders get pumped out of the gate and start doing all the right things—

scrimmaging once a week as a team, conducting coaching one-on-one sessions, and really focusing on growing each team member. But then, like a child with a new toy, we feel the newness and fun start to wear off, and so does the excitement. There should be no excuses for not seeing and anticipating this. We know this will happen, sometimes within weeks. It *will* happen, and we must be prepared to avoid the trap.

The best exit strategy from Trap #1 is to stay committed to things like scrimmaging and team recognition and reward programs by getting your team involved more and more in planning and executing them. Be careful not to cop out and delegate your coaching activities: Don't delegate actions to someone else because it bores you. Do that, and you rip off your team, depriving them of what they deserve—your time and commitment. And then, even if you think your team is great, don't stop doing the right things.

Trap #2: My Team Is Already Great

I have four children, and I can honestly say they are all perfect. My oldest is wicked smart. My eleven-year-old daughter has one of the biggest hearts and generous souls of anyone you have ever met. My three-year-old has the most magnetic energy and a presence that makes you love her. My two-year-old is beautiful and the strongest two-year-old girl I have ever seen. If my praise sounds familiar to you, you are probably parents saying the same things about your kids, or the friend of those parents who wishes they would shut up about their kids. Either way, you know what I mean: Sometimes leaders, like parents, take this hyperbolic see-no-imperfections attitude toward their team. Maybe we feel obligated to sing their praises in the way parents do their kids. Or maybe we think, "Well, duh. They're on my team. Of course they're awesome."

There may be kids out there smarter and more gifted than my kids, prettier than my daughters and more handsome than my son, but my kids are my family and I can't replace them. Unlike with family, as a business leader, you *cannot get attached to an idealized version of your team.* We must ask, "Who on my team is not performing to the team standards?" Then we need to move them up to the standards. Then raise the standards.

In professional sports, teams draft new and more talented players every year, not because they hate their current team or don't think they're any good but because their job is to find the best talent and place them on the team. In business, we must remember: Everyone is replaceable. Yes, this is a harsh reality, but it is a real one: *Everyone is valuable but not necessary.* Be willing and able to look at your team subjectively and ask some hard questions regularly:

- Can this person take our team to the next level?
- If I left the company, which of them would I want to take over the team?

It is normal for leaders to respect and care about their teams, especially those who have been with us for a long time, but everybody must still earn their roster spot *every year.* Don't allow personal emotions to keep you from making the best professional decisions. Doing the right thing is sometimes hard, but never wrong.

Trap #3: Checking the Box

This trap could also be called the going-through-the-motions trap. It is too easy to do a task and check the box merely to say that we have done it. We may not even realize we've fallen into this trap. But the consequences for trapped coaches can be especially drastic if the team follows like lemmings.

What are the signs of this trap? We start having scrimmages just to have them or give a game ball just to do something. We stop planning even for the most important activities. I recently had a client call me on a Friday morning to tell me he was about to have his weekly practice and was trying to throw together his agenda real quick—just minutes before the meeting. We all have done this at one time or another, but **we cannot stop giving the same amount of respect and dedication to the coaching of our teams that we want our teams to give to us.** That's checking the box, and often the first step to stopping these activities.

This is no different from what happens every spring when I bring our boat to the house for spring cleaning. My kids *love* this day (not), and everyone has a job. After about twenty minutes, my oldest daughter, who is tasked with cleaning the seats, says, "Daddy, I'm done."

"No way you cleaned all of those seats that fast," I tell her. She very confidently responds, "Yes, I did; look for yourself." Turns out, she did exactly what she thought was right: She put cleaner on one of the seats and wiped it onto every seat. Every seat was wiped but far from clean, and some were dirtier than others. I took this as a teachable moment. I took the cleaner and started to clean one of the front seats. I sprayed and scrubbed and sprayed and scrubbed. My seat was really clean and I asked my daughter, "Do you see a difference in the seat I cleaned and the ones you cleaned?" She said, "Yes, but that is because you are bigger and stronger." I said, "Not really, honey; the reason is that our intentions are different. I am cleaning the seat with the intention and goal to make this seat look brand-new, and your intention or goal was just to get it done."

The only way to avoid checking the box is to make sure we are involved as much as possible so that we hold ourselves accountable in front of our teams. Recommit to coaching the team with the intention that you will make them better every week, every month, and every year, with the goal to help them grow and grow their careers. Coach with great intent and you will gain great players.

Trap #4: Allowing Bottom Performers to Leave on Their Own Timeline

We've talked a lot about focusing on top performers and dealing with decent performers who have bad attitudes. But that does not mean leaders can focus only on these people and let our poorest performers decide on their own to leave the company rather than our taking the initiative to usher them out the door. Taking that easy way out and lapsing back into the selfish, conflict-avoiding, unaccountable management culture when dealing with underperformers sends a message that is more important than the action. It also leads to a crisis of sorts: By the time underperforming employees make the decision to leave, they'll most likely have taken their quality of work down to rock bottom, and the other team members will have noticed it. This sends a message to others that we don't value those who go beyond and do their best. Now it's the company, not the underperforming employee, who looks suspect.

If poor performers are leaving of their own volition, then something must be wrong with the coach and the organization, not just the person: "She made the decision to leave, not her boss, so I bet she's right." It's good to give underperformers a chance to improve before showing them the door, but what we cannot do is allow underperformance to become acceptable and turn into the status quo. Don't wait for anyone to leave of his or her own accord. **Hire fast, fire faster, and hold everyone accountable no matter how much conflict ensues.**

Trap #5: Not Believing

This trap can be the cause of much heartbreak and brings us back to where we started and into the final part of the book. I call this trap the "I don't believe we can, but I don't believe my team knows that, so it's okay" trap. Here's how it goes. Leaders set logical goals for their teams and tell the team members that they can achieve them, but they don't really believe the members have it in them to do so. Then the leaders' interactions betray their infidelity: Belief can't be faked, not long-term at least, and not in the dynamic of team interaction.

Trust me, just as our kids know when we are not being truthful, so do our teams. As leaders, we not only need a play-to-win mentality but also have to believe it. If we lack faith in our teams to win, then we shouldn't be leading them. No matter the business or sport, no team or athlete can show up expecting to lose. That's as much a reflection of the coach as anything else. In becoming coaches, leaders are given greater challenges than they have faced in the past and, at first glance, can feel overwhelmed and have doubts. That's okay, but remember to be logical, not realistic, even when it comes to the act of coaching itself. None of what we have covered in this book is easy. Some of it may seem far from realistic at times, but I assure you, the only thing that keeps anything from being possible in coaching is not believing in your team and not making that team believe in themselves.

Don't ignore the obstacles or the enormous challenges you are facing; strive to overcome them and you will achieve great-

166 | **NATHAN JAMAIL**

ness. Remember: An obstacle in business can be as easy to get around as a closed street in your hometown, or as difficult as keeping your kids out of harm's way. Belief is a choice—the essential choice in coaching. So what is yours?

Takeaways:
Avoiding the Biggest Management Traps

- Always mandate coaching activities and skills of coaching for your team and yourself.
- Sustain the coaching activities and actions you have put in place.
- Be proud of your team but don't have an idealized vision of them.
- Hire fast, fire faster.
- Always believe in what you preach and do.

PART
THREE
Create a Coaching Culture

Chapter 10

THE DESIRE TO WIN

To succeed as coaches, leaders need a culture that supports the activities of coaching.

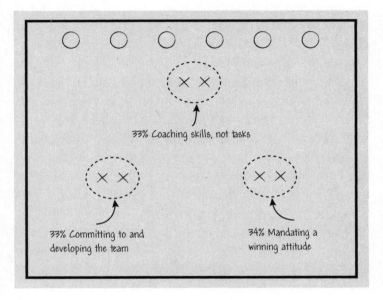

33% Coaching skills, not tasks

33% Committing to and developing the team

34% Mandating a winning attitude

A client asked me the other day, "What's more important, winning or not losing?" At first, I thought, *Winning.* Then, I answered something different: "The desire to win." Yes, I want the people who work for me to think like Dale Earnhardt, who said, "Second place is just the first-place *loser.*" I want my team to say, "We are going to win every race, and if we lose, we just ran out of time." But coaches know this desire to win comes from more than the activities and actions of coaching. No coach or superstar athlete can win it all alone. They need a team that shares their desire, improves their skills, and has something more—a culture that supports a desire to win and fields winning teams with winning attitudes year after year. That's how great sports franchises and dynasties are made: They build on a winning *mind-set*.

In business, it is the same. It is not enough that leaders know *how* to coach and develop the skills and activities of coaching if they, their bosses, and the organization don't embrace a culture that supports the change from managing to coaching. Understanding and implementing the principles, actions, and activities of coaching, such as scrimmaging, peer presentations, and logical goals, have the *potential* to create, develop, and grow winning teams, but they are only part of what turns great leaders into great coaches. Winning coaches, teams, and organizations must also have winning mind-sets that, top to bottom, mandate the belief in a desire to win, hold people accountable for it, and force leaders to get more involved with the teams to maintain it.

Those are the essential, highly integrated characteristics of a coaching culture we cover in this part of the book—the desire to win, accountability, and getting "on the field" with your team. Leaders who are coaches know *their number one priority is to coach their teams,* which means *working with them to make them better* as a team. And success comes down to one essential principle: **Leaders expect only what we inspect; if we don't inspect it, don't expect it.**

I'll say it one last time: One of the greatest mistakes leaders make in business today is to live by a philosophy of "I hire great people and get out of their way so they can do their jobs." That's why managers in management cultures don't coach much, if at all: The culture of the organization does not support the depth of involvement needed to coach, let alone mandate it. Time-consuming coaching activities, the constant need to motivate the team and improve morale, and the inevitable conflict that arises from making the tough decisions to coach people up or out of the organization—and holding *ourselves* accountable for all of it? That can add up to one huge ineffective beatdown for leaders.

The Desire to Win Starts with a Desire to Get Involved

Once, in the middle of a presentation I was making about coaches getting involved and the desire to win, the founder and CEO of the company stood up and said, "I don't think I agree with you. I pay my people to do their jobs and think for themselves, not to have me constantly micromanaging and telling them how to do it."

"I appreciate that," I said. "You make a valid point. But I want you to consider another way of looking at it. To grow and develop our people, we want them to benefit from our experience and know we support them. We want them striving for more and not be left to wonder if they are doing the right things. Yes, they need to express their own creativity and be allowed to make mistakes and grow without hand-holding. But even leaders need and want leadership, and as their coaches, we should be there to guide, encourage, and push them—and then mandate that they do the same for the teams who report to them, and so on."

My point wasn't to challenge the CEO or to be disrespectful. I wasn't telling this CEO to hire people who wait for him to tell them what's right and what to do. I believe in creating a team of people who push themselves and go out and take chances and make big decisions—who may sometimes screw up big but will always ultimately succeed big. I simply wanted to get him to stop confusing the more micro involvement of coaching activities with micromanaging.

Look at it this way. If I could show the people who work for me how to make a million dollars a month for my company, would I:

(A) want them to figure it out on their own?
(B) give them the *Reader's Digest* version of it and then leave them alone?
(C) tell them how to do it, step by step, and then stay involved to push and encourage them to succeed?

Of course, the answer should be C. Who better to do this than you? I say we give our teams all the tools, direction, leadership, and depth of our experience and put them in the best possible position to succeed. As a leader, I have the ability and the responsibility to instill a desire to win by putting my team in the position to win with support, guidance, and encouragement.

Leaders might be concerned if we spend all this time coaching the top people; those people are just going to leave and take what they learned somewhere else to compete against us. Come on, we give ourselves way too much credit. *Nobody's that smart or that good.* That's useless worrying. We will benefit from a top performer's work as much as they benefit from our knowledge.

Simply put, stop thinking that someone recruiting from your team is a bad thing when it is actually *a great thing*—even if it is a client of yours or a potential business partner. The more people who work for us and are coached by us to a new level with a deep desire to win, and who then get recruited from our teams for better jobs, the stronger our network becomes and the better we can build our team's reputation for creating winners. Those former employees know that we made them better, and that's the foundation for extremely powerful relationships that never expire.

Or just think of it the way my client, Ken Smith, vice president of North American Field Sales and Region Development at Georgia Pacific, does: "What if we didn't train these people and didn't invest in them and they *stayed*!"

Coaches get involved in the beginning and micromanagers get involved in the end.

Micromanaging versus Getting Involved

Merriam-Webster defines *micromanage* as "to try to control or manage all the small parts of (something, such as an activity) in a way that is usually not wanted or that causes problems." After all we have covered here, does that sound like what coaches do when performing the activities of coaching? That's not the kind of involvement and direction that leads to top performance and a desire to win. Sports teams and their superstars don't resent the involvement of the coaches who help them win, so why should the people who work for us? Because managers who are not involved with their teams tend to get involved only when there is a problem. And as we discussed briefly in Part One, we can't coach a team that always views our involvement in the negative.

For example, I was leading a coaching workshop for vice presidents at a Fortune 100 financial company about the need to get involved to develop their teams of agents, when one of them said, "I don't worry about my people's activity until the results are bad. As long as the numbers are good, I don't break down activity. I break it down when things are bad." That's exactly what leads to micromanaging: getting involved only in the negative. If I manage activity solely as a response to people not doing their jobs or not achieving results, then all my involvement will be perceived as micromanaging.

The goal of coaching isn't to make bad teams good; it is to make any team better. Coaches should *never* use activity as a consequence; we should use activity to prepare our teams to win and then give feedback when the results are bad *and* good. We should be a part of most scrimmages. We should go to meetings and appointments to find out what our teams are doing. We should then give them feedback on what we found and develop the skills they need to perform better, or move them out if we think they can't perform. In other words, coaching involvement through activity management is not just about what we do—it's *when and why* we do it. A micromanager inspects because he doesn't think a person is able or capable to do the job without help. A coach inspects to help develop and prepare the team to do their jobs better.

To Win, Coach Skills, Not Tasks

Understanding how to get involved comes from knowing *what* to coach. Many times, leaders will pick out tasks for employees, focus on "training" them in how to do those tasks better, and think they are "coaching" their people. Tasks are not skills; tasks are, well, tasks. It's one thing to know the tasks you have to do; it's quite another to have developed the skills necessary to do these and other tasks well. Typically, in business, when we are teaching our people how to do their jobs or specific tasks, we call this training. When we coach, we are working with our team members on communication skills, leadership, influence, motivation, energy . . . all the skills and attributes that make people better professionals and enable them to work together as a team. This can be not only hard to do but also harder for the organization to justify the time commitment when these skills are not necessarily tangible ROI items. But this is exactly the reason people don't grow and develop a desire to win—there is no culture that mandates it.

A multimillion-dollar client of mine in the construction business had an issue with its site manager at a shopping center who was in charge of installing the underground equipment for the entire project. This site manager knew everything in the world about pipes and pipe installation, but he lacked the ability to work and communicate well with the other companies on the job site. Everyone hated him, and my client was suffering because of it. For example, one day, the site manager needed to make sure a pipe was installed before another company did their site work. But because the other company did not like the site manager and had no agreement with my client's company to partner on that work, the other company went ahead and built their section without letting my client know. My client now had to find a way to work around this issue, and it led to two days in delays and increased labor and material costs.

Construction is more than just building.

But as much as this was a reflection on the unlikability of the site manager, the bigger picture had less to do with the site manager and everything to do with leadership, namely addressing the site manager's inability to manage effective business relationships. Thus, the issue with this project had been managed as a result but never *coached* so it would not happen again. If the issue had been coached, the leader of *all* the site managers would have anticipated situations like this and done mock scrimmages multiple times on how to build effective relationships on the job site, instead of waiting until there was a problem and then attempting to fix it. My client would have solved a problem before it happened or at least known that the site manager needed help solving it. **That is the mind-set of a coach in a coaching cul-**

176 | NATHAN JAMAIL

ture: **getting involved before there is a problem, getting involved to win by focusing on what matters most—our people.**

Focus on the Roots, Not the Fruits

Too often, leaders focus on revenue, sales, product development, customer service, employee satisfaction, etc., as issues disconnected from our people. But as we discussed in Chapter 6, they are fruits of our labor and efforts. They cannot fully be achieved without focusing on the roots of our business—our people. When we focus on our team members' skills (the roots), they will continue to bear great results (the fruits). And I believe all business leaders, even if they were chosen by default, *can* do this regardless of their own skill set, as long as they have the mind-set and develop their skills as coaches.

Coaches don't have to have better skills than the team.

At the start of this book, I said that one of the main reasons leaders don't coach their people is that they are afraid to find out that those people are not as good as they thought. But actually, there is a more selfish fear: We think, by coaching, we will be "found out" that we are not as good as some, if not all, of our players. But what coach is? Hank Haney couldn't hit a ball farther than Tiger Woods. Bill Belichick can't throw a pass like Tom Brady. Even good players who became incredibly successful coaches, such as Phil Jackson in the NBA or Pat Summitt at the University of Tennessee, never had the skills of their superstars. Superstars in most sports sometimes become coaches, but more often, they become consultants and business board members. The greatest sports coaches (or even the good ones who are not Hall of Famers) can coach those superstars with confidence and a winning attitude without ever worrying they need to prove something as their equals. Do you think Michael Phelps did not listen to Bob Bowman because Bowman never made it beyond his college swim team? Béla Károlyi competed in the hammer throw, not gymnastics. Did that stop Nadia Comăneci or Mary Lou Retton from listening to him and getting perfect tens? What makes leaders in business think this way? A coach's job isn't to be as good as the team. A coach's job is to make the team and all its players better than they were yesterday.

At Sprint, I knew a twenty-one-year-old who, we felt, despite her age, had the desire to win and a coaching mind-set. She had done excellent work as an assistant manager of a thriving large retail store that had once struggled. So Sprint promoted her to manager of an equally large store that resembled hers before the turnaround and was in dire need of a new direction. Moments into her first day on the job, that store's assistant manager, who felt she had been passed over for the store manager job, made it very clear that she didn't think the new "young" manager could do anything better than she could.

I asked the new manager how she handled this rebuke, and she said that she recognized the victim disease (which we covered in Chapter 8) in the assistant manager right away. Feeling you get passed over for a job—and using that as an excuse to be negative, unmotivated, and unsuccessful—is something victims do. *No one* gets "passed over" for a job. That assistant manager was simply not the best fit and the right person for the job at the time. That doesn't mean the person *couldn't be* the right person eventually, but she would never get there without being coached to have a desire to win that turns victims into victors. So the new manager confronted the assistant manager to see if this was possible.

"Let me ask you, do you think this store can perform better than it is?" she asked the assistant manager.

"Nope. It is in a bad location. There is never enough inventory, the staff is not very good, and our coverage is worse," replied the assistant manager.

"Anything else?" the new manager asked.

"The demographics are all wrong in this market and our phones are terrible," added the assistant manager.

"Well, then, you are right. It can't perform better," she said. "Not with those beliefs."

What the new manager had quickly realized is that things would never get better, not because of the obstacles the assistant manager mentioned but because the assistant manager believed those obstacles could not be overcome. Now, some of this was obviously resentment and venting because she did not get the job, but the assistant manager continued to believe those obstacles couldn't be overcome days and weeks later. Meanwhile, the new store manager never stopped believing they could be overcome and was prepared to make the team believe it too. She came into the failing store and said, "At my other store, we faced the same issues we face here and we were getting terrific results when I left. That means that WE can get these results." There would be hard work involved, as she acknowledged, but she genuinely believed success would come and had a leadership plan that included revitalizing the team, developing each player, and expecting everyone (including the assistant manager) to have a positive attitude and a desire to win. She did not believe the past should predict their future. What had been good enough was no longer good; it was unacceptable. That's what sparked a change in the attitude of the entire team. She reset the expectations.

One of the first things she implemented as part of her coaching were regular practice and scrimmaging sessions to develop the team based on what she found as she got involved. As the manager learned where a problem existed with the store or the team, the next day, that problem or skill would become part of practice sessions, weekly scrimmage meetings, and one-on-one meetings. Sometimes, because of the need to solve an urgent problem or issues at a specific location performance, they were done immediately, off the floor, even in the stockroom. They scrimmaged simple, basic things like customer greetings and how to pay attention to the customer you are with while acknowledging the ones coming in the door (greeting them within three seconds by saying "excuse me" to the existing customer and telling the new ones you will be right with them). They scrimmaged how to make people feel welcome in person and on the phone. Soon, they worked up to presenting new information (plans, phones, and coverage maps) and anticipating customer questions so they could immediately understand those customers' perspectives and establish trust and influence.

The manager held all team members accountable for these scrimmages and the broader plan. Through the scrimmages alone, the team and the store started to improve. She asked them to commit to the team and told the poorest performers, "Change your beliefs or we change you"—including the assistant manager who had not been promoted. Employees who wanted to be part of the team went from just showing up every morning and "doing their jobs" to practicing certain skills together. Unfortunately, the assistant manager didn't get any better. She rejected the coaching efforts of the new manager, telling her that scrimmaging wouldn't work. When the manager tried to implement a change, the assistant manager made sure to tell her that wasn't how they used to do it, citing this as a reason not to change.

Now, you don't need to work in a store or sales to recognize this kind of person—someone who makes every obstacle an ex-

> **Experience is a negative when it limits you from believing what you can achieve.**

cuse for what can't or couldn't be done. Every one of my clients, from the military, insurance, energy, technology, manufacturing, and beyond, has had an employee like this who uses excuses to keep them and the team from having a positive attitude and achieving their goals. Walk into any store or any department in any office, and if the energy is negative and the people aren't polite, go find their leader. I promise you will find the problem, because that leader will be just like them. Very rarely do you see a positive, strong, committed leader in charge of a low-performing negative team. The reverse is true too—you won't find high-performing, positive, and driven teams working for negative, unmotivated "managers," which was exactly the case in the Sprint store. Think about that when you picture the perception of your teams.

It should come as no surprise that the assistant manager at that Sprint store was soon fired. The excuses never stopped. She was uncoachable. She would not go from victim to victor, and the manager knew she would not get better, so she had the tough conversation. In fact, half the staff left, and it took weeks and months to make all the changes the new manager wanted. But by addressing the assistant manager directly, it made everyone who stayed realize that excuses were not going to be accepted anymore, because the lead excuse maker was now gone. Those excuses were now just obstacles to resolve and remove by the leader with her team. She showed the team how to believe in themselves and that translated into everything they did. Six months in, her store became the number one performing store in the district.

In the end, it did not matter that the new manager was only

twenty-one years old, or had less retail experience than the assistant manager or other team members. She wasn't the best inventory manager or cashier. She didn't need to be. She simply made
sure the people responsible for those jobs were, and mandated
top performance and practice from all of them. As leaders, we
want our employees to know more about their jobs than we do
and come up with ways to do them even better. It doesn't matter
if the people on the team are older, better-looking, more popular,
have more experience or tenure, are better at certain skills, and
smarter than us (trust me on the smarter part). None of those
things are or should be qualifications for being a coach or being
successful as a coach.

Think of it this way: It wasn't Paul McCartney, Sting, Bono,
or Phil Collins who wrote "Do They Know It's Christmas?" and
invited all those superstars to create Band Aid in 1984 and raised
millions for children starving in Africa. It was Bob Geldof of the
Boomtown Rats and Midge Ure of Ultravox. Even though most
of the performers they recruited were probably better and certainly more famous songwriters, musicians, and singers than
they were, Geldof and Ure were the ones who pulled it all together and made it happen. They made the team believe they
could do it, motivated them to want to be a part of it, gave them
the song to do it with, and inspired countless projects like it that
have made the world a better place for decades since.

Takeaways:
The Desire to Win

- The desire to win and the belief in winning is
  essential for a coach to succeed.
- Inspect what you expect.
- Coach skills, not tasks.

- Leaders gets paid to coach and develop their people regardless of title, department, or industry.
- A coach does not have to be better than the player to make the player better.

Chapter 11
A CULTURE OF ACCOUNTABILITY

By not holding our people accountable, we selfishly say to them, "You're just not worth the trouble."

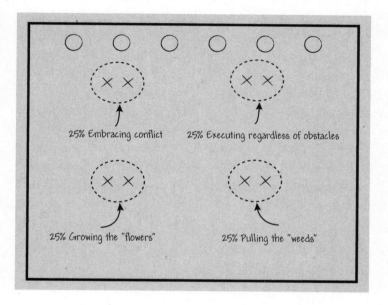

My father and I had just attended an event and decided to get lunch at a restaurant we didn't know but was right across the street. Both of us agreed the food was not very good—edible but not good. Just then, the manager walked by and asked how everything was and if we were enjoying our meals. We both looked at him and said, "It's great." Sound familiar? Of course it does. Truth is, we are really lousy at holding people accountable for a poor performance, especially when the stakes are not high. I'm not above this. I couldn't even tell a manager I didn't know in a restaurant I had never been, and likely would never go into again, that I didn't like the food. Day in and day out, no one tells us we suck.

In business, it is even worse. Why is it so hard to establish a culture of accountability, and coach people to be better? Why do we always wait until the end of the year to evaluate someone, dreading every moment until it comes? *Because we are selfish.* Leaders say it's because they're nice and trust their teams to do their jobs, but they really don't want to deal with all the pain of accountability and getting involved. That's not nice; it's selfish. That's not trust; it's abdication of responsibility for the success of the team, especially of our top performers. It's also lazy and being scared about what we might find if we take the time to coach—we don't want to deal with what comes next, so we don't. **But we must mandate this accountability if we want coaching to succeed in our organizations, because accountability makes good employees better and makes bad employees leave.**

Demand Accountability

Let's put this selfish management philosophy into a sports analogy. The Indianapolis Colts drafted Andrew Luck out of Stanford to be the heir apparent to Peyton Manning. Luck showed up on day one of training camp and his coach said, "Luck, I draft great people and I get out of their way. So here is what we are going to do: I'll walk you around the stadium here. I'll show you where the locker room, training facilities, equipment, and parking garage are. I'll get you set up with a uniform and equipment, give you the playbook, and then you can go off and run some drills on your own to get ready. Great to have you on board. Really excited we got you. I'll see you Sunday."

There is no way any coach in professional sports would ever do that with any draft pick, let alone their top draft pick. Andrew Luck is going to be on the field every day, practicing harder than everyone to get better, and his coach is going to be watching him every minute to make sure of it—just as he did with Peyton Manning before him (and that turned out pretty well for them). The coach is going to hold Luck accountable to develop his skills and to commit to the team.

Yet, in business, we hire someone like Andrew Luck, train him, and let him "do his job." No skill development or talk about committing to the team. We say it is because we trust him, but really we *don't want to do the work.* That's lazy *and* crazy.

When I tell leaders this, from the stage, they can't agree more. They say, "Amen, brother Nathan!" They love the idea. But when we finish and I say, "What are you going to do on Monday?" They say, "I am going to do a practice meeting and start . . ." and suddenly the energy leaves the room. They quickly realize that the easy part of coaching is the energy. The hard part is the effort. It's like raising kids: It's amazing how much love and passion we have for them, but the actual work of raising children is brutal. Yet we will hold our kids to standards that we wouldn't even bring up with an employee, especially a veteran one. **We will hold a ten-year-old to a higher standard than we will hold an adult to whom we pay tens of thousands of dollars per year.**

> Demanding accountability in everything that we do and ask the team to do as leaders is essential to our success.

An employee walks up to a customer and is rude? Doesn't dress right? Shows up late? We would never let our kids get away with that. You know why? The intent of why we are doing it. We love our kids so much, and we are scared to death that when they go out in public and do something wrong, it is a direct reflection on us as the parents. And worse: We are scared they will become unproductive adults in the long run. So we hold them accountable. We ground them. We take away their electronics or the car, even though that only makes us suffer because now we have to hear how they "have nothing to do," and we can't send them to the store because we just took away the car. Grounding kids is miserable for parents, but we do it because our intent is to make our kids the best human beings we possibly can. In business, too many leaders just don't care enough about their people when they do things like that. We think, *They're our responsibility, but they're not our kids, so they are not worth all that effort.* We think, *That's a hard conversation to have and it's only going to lead to those people defending themselves over and over and saying they didn't do it. I get enough of that at home.*

Don't get me wrong: I'm not using parenting analogies in this chapter to say our employees are children or that we act like children. I'm saying it is easy to be a manager who lets performance slide, hiding behind the idea that we should hire good people and stay out of their way. If you're like me, you remember your best leaders, teachers, and coaches pushing you harder than anyone else. They helped shape me, challenged me to be my best self, and held me to a standard higher than the standard to which I held myself. They stopped me in my tracks when I made a small but important mistake, because they knew that small mistake could be the difference between winning and losing. But they truly cared for me—and what they did too. Love guided their desire to hold me accountable to learn and grow. I want leaders to remember what it is like to give and receive that extra push to do what we know we *should* do.

Consider these questions:

- Have you ever been grateful that someone just quit so you didn't have to deal with the person anymore?
- Have you ever treated an employee like someone you were dating and wanted to break up with, but instead of doing it, you avoided him or her?
- Have you ever become less attentive, instituted certain "rules," and maybe even acted a little bit like a jerk—but not hostile—so an employee would "get the message" and quit?

If we can answer yes to any of these questions, then we have acted selfishly as leaders, avoiding conflict rather than embracing it. It really *is* us, not them. We *must* coach our teams and hold them accountable in the same way the best parents and sports coaches do—not to micromanage, stifle creativity, or take their authority, but to push them to be better and win. That's what I did with the top performer who was sucking the life out of my team in Chapter 7. That's what the store manager did with the staff that wanted to do better in the previous chapter. And it worked because we had a culture of accountability to back us up. That's why accountability is *mandatory*; it may most often lead to coaching people off the team, but it starts with a desire to win and make *everybody* better. Plus, the replacements for the people lost will more than make up for any perceived loss, since the new people are coming into a culture that mandates coaching and believes it *is* worth the time and effort.

Inspect What You Expect: Grow the Flowers

One of my favorite parts about coaching leaders is asking them questions like:

- Are you better today than you were sixty days ago? How about a year ago?
- Are your people simply more tenured or actually better? What have you really taught them?
- What can you say they have done that they couldn't do before? How have you made someone better?

No leader can answer these questions positively or at all without a culture that mandates full accountability and focuses on making the team better.

Now, think about each person on your team. Knowing them as you do today, would you rehire them yourself for a new company tomorrow? Be honest and be tough. If you said "No" or "Probably not," then you have a problem. Now let me ask you this: Do these people know you feel this way? If you said "No" or "Probably not," then you have an even bigger problem. In most management cultures, employees don't know how their leaders feel, even when we think they do or should. So here's my challenge to you: Within forty-eight hours from the time you put this book down, meet with a person you would not hire again, let him or her know how you feel, and for sixty days, coach this person into the applicant you *would* hire so you can answer the first question above "Yes!" Before you say you can't do it, consider this: If your boss thought this way about you, would you want him or her to tell you?

Put together a plan using the principles and playbook from

the first parts of this book, then scrimmage the conversation a few times before you sit down with the employee. You can start by simply saying, "Unaccountable Person, I value you and want you to be happy here. I have been pondering each person on my team, and when I think about you and your [performance, attitude, actions], I realize you can't truly be happy at this moment, for you are not performing up to the full potential I need and require. I have some thoughts on how you can get there, but I first want to know from you if you want to perform to your full potential." If the employee fails to say yes or doesn't want to meet your expectations, then it's time to fire this person or move him or her to a different job that is a better fit.

This might sound hard-nosed, but it is not. It *is* hard-nosed and downright mean to let that person stay in that position. The employee may be flabbergasted. After all, you have never held him or her accountable for these issues until now. That's okay. This is not necessarily a time for corrective action; this is a time to discuss how you see the employee's position and what you would like to see, moving forward. Make sure you scrimmage and prepare for these meetings with someone you trust prior to each conversation you have. If you do this with each person you wouldn't rehire, here is my promise: You will be amazed at the response, and even pleasantly surprised by some of the turnarounds. Your team will always be better for the weeds you would have pulled anyway, but it will thrive with the flowers that grow in their place.

Inspect What You Expect: Pull the Weeds

I used to go into meetings with a struggling employee, planning to have a constructive conversation and set an ultimatum: The employee must start doing better or he will be terminated.

Instead, I left the meeting with an action list of all the things I needed to do for this employee to whom I *gave* the ultimatum! Many leaders laugh at this statement when I use it in my speeches because they know it happens all the time. Well, here is the good news: A coach who leads in a culture that mandates accountability will *not* let that happen again.

First, let's look at how it happens. It starts somewhere in the meeting, usually after I've pointed out to the employee all the things he needs to improve on, and then I say something like "Now tell me, Mr.-Struggling-Employee-I-Have-Never-Held-Accountable-for-Anything, what can I do for you to help you meet these expectations?" That's when the floodgates of excuses open and all the issues I discussed with this employee become *my* issues and are likely viewed as *my* fault. The employee leaves still unaccountable for his problems and I am left with a to-do list.

For example, I was in a corrective action meeting with one of my sales managers, discussing his lack of performance, his lack of attention to detail, and his unwillingness to focus on his team's development. I had several specific examples of situations in which he did not perform the required practice meetings with his team and did not hold certain team members accountable for their actions. And then it happened. I asked him the deadly diversion question, "So you know what I expect from you moving forward; what can I do to help you do your job better?" Boy, did he tell me. According to him, I could remove this task and this report, attend to another manager who wasn't doing his job, eliminate some of the practice sessions, and so on and so on. By the end of the meeting, I had postponed the intended written warning so I could research these obstacles for him and help him meet my expectations. He walked off without being held accountable for one thing on my list.

Fortunately, I worked in a culture that expected accountability, and my boss helped me learn from that mistake by understanding what I know now: It's not our job to remove all or any of our team's obstacles; it is our job to coach them to become bigger than the obstacles.

To stop this process, don't ever ask employees, "What can I do for you?" Meetings like these are about *their* performance. After we clarify all the expectations and identify what behaviors or results must change, ask these questions instead:

- Given this information, do you think you will be able to achieve these expectations?
- What will you have to do differently to reach these expectations?

Then, let the employee speak, if for no other reason than to appreciate and come to terms with the gravity of the situation. They are there to justify their continued employment, not ours. Don't leave this or any meeting with a handful of vague promises. Make sure the employee has a clear understanding of how to succeed, and be prepared to deal with what happens if they don't. Accountability may start with embracing conflict, but it fails when we don't have a plan in place to deal with what we are holding the team accountable for.

This is where building your bench (Chapter 6) is particularly important. If a person doesn't improve, we go through the disciplinary steps of verbal warning, written warning, a final written warning, an "I really mean it now" final written warning (as my good friend, Jim Moreland, used to say, "Let's throw ugly on the table too"), and then termination. But now finding a quality replacement takes additional time and resources, and getting new staff up to speed takes yet more of our time. If we always had a top-quality person ready to take the place of all our bad performers, would we be more willing to hold our people accountable? Yes! The best time to interview for future employees is when we don't need one. But let me also make it clear: We are better off with an open spot than with a bad performer, no matter the job. I say this with the humble heart of someone who continues to struggle with all of this: Know what is right and you win every time. I have done it wrong. I have used all of the readily available excuses for not holding people accountable myself. And I know those excuses were a lot easier to make when the organization around me did not mandate that I hold those people accountable and be a coach. **So suck it up and pull the weeds and watch your flowers grow.**

Takeaways:
Accountability

- Don't be selfish: If a person has a bad attitude, that is their problem. If we are paying them and not holding them accountable, that is our fault!
- A coach's job is to hire good people and constantly make them better.
- Getting involved is NOT mircomanaging—it cannot be unwanted, happen only when things go wrong, and it must happen with the intent of helping a team member get better.
- Inspect what you expect: You can't have accountability by just letting people do their jobs.

Chapter 12
GET ON THE FIELD

We can't coach from our desks.

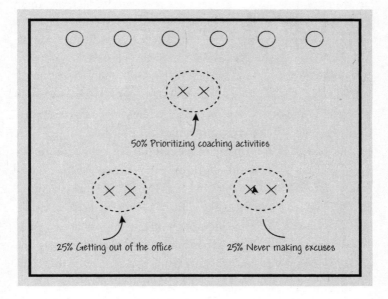

A top energy industry executive I once coached loved working with his team, but for reasons seemingly out of his control, he found himself stuck in his office or in meetings, not out with the team where he wanted and loved to be. He had found great success getting involved with his teams in the past, but now that he had moved all the way up the corporate ladder to CEO, he had ended up doing what most executives do: Visit an office or plant when there was an event at which he needed to make an appearance or when there was a major issue that demanded his presence and immediate attention. He was never there just to *be there* as an ongoing part of his job.

This is a fairly typical situation in many organizations: The higher we move up in the corporate structure, the more difficult it becomes to get out from behind our desks, not just because of added responsibilities and titles but because there is no one there to make us do it. This is not just about management cultures versus coaching cultures; it's about no one mandating what we already know we should do. Boards of directors are not going to tell their CEOs to get out of their offices and "on the field." Thus, in most cases, the CEOs are not telling their VPs to do that either and so those VPs have no reason to hold their direct reports accountable until the company mandates it.

But leaders can't fully inspect what we expect from behind our desks and the doors of our offices. That's exactly why one of the first things I made this CEO do was get out of his office (and away from the screens on his computer, tablet, and phone) and into the field, meaning any place that work was being done by his team. He initially pushed back, citing the usual reasons I had heard before, such as a bunch of meetings and the need to put out some fires, but what I needed him to see was what we covered in chapters 8 and 11: These were *obstacles* (facts we must and can overcome, such as competition, inventory, too many appointments and fires to put out) being turned into *excuses* (what we say is the reason for not overcoming the obstacle, achieving our goals, or doing something we want).

CEOs are not immune to doing this, because it is pretty easy to do: Just personalize the obstacle. "We would have done that but . . . The competition did this so I couldn't . . . The economy did such-and-such, which really made it difficult to . . . You don't understand: It is different in this market, which is why I can't . . ." These are all obstacles turned into excuses rather than into solutions.

Obstacle to Not Getting on the Field	Excuse for Not Getting on the Field
People are spread out all over the country.	I can't possibly take the time to visit everyone spread throughout the company, let alone the country.
Other tasks have more immediate impact on the business.	I need to focus on the tasks at hand.
Expectations are for me to focus on the big picture and handle big problems.	I have a team of leaders to tell me what is happening on the field.
I'm too busy handling problems and putting out fires.	I can't get in the field because I am paid to fix problems and put out fires.

I'm not saying we *have* to overcome these obstacles to be great leaders. I'm saying that if leaders want to be great coaches, they have to overcome these obstacles and get out there more. Sure, the bigger the title, the more people reporting to us; the more responsibilities, distractions, and problems we have; but bigger obstacles don't need bigger solutions—they need better priorities.

We Can't "Fit In" Coaching

My point was not to tell my CEO client or anyone I work with that they are not doing their jobs correctly. I am trying to get them to look in the mirror and say: "Am I really doing what I need to do to develop and lead my team or am I focusing on short-term issues, things that bring instant gratification and paths of least resistance?" It is absolutely true that leaders are paid to do the activities and actions that we describe as obstacles to coaching. But that's not all we get paid to do; that's only part of our job.

From the bottom of an organization to the top, everyone is paid to do multiple jobs. The people at the reception desk are paid to greet and sign in visitors and answer the phones, but they also clean the counters, direct deliveries, call for messengers, and coordinate maintenance and other building activities for the office. To get it all done, this person must prioritize what matters most and when. For leaders in business, it is the same: If we want to be coaches, what matters most must be coaching and the coaching activities that make our teams better. Coaches get paid to develop, grow, and lead their teams, not to attend to the publicity people, reporters, recruiters, team manager, team owner, affiliates, branding specialists, administration, or rehab departments, unless those are one of the teams they are leading. Coaches set the thermostat for morale. They motivate, scrimmage, reward, peer-present, and review the game plans.

We need to prioritize and make coaching the core of our leadership so that everything *else* fits *around* it—and the culture of the organization must mandate that priority. Here is a good rule of thumb: If you manage managers (i.e., if you are CEO, president, VP, or director level) and you aspire to be a leader and a coach, then *you need to be out there anywhere from 40 to 80 percent of your time* performing the activities of coaching, and mandate that those who report to you do the same with their teams.

Make the time to be out there—prioritize coaching.

Yes, the instant gratification of clearing our in-box or desk feels good. But it is part of a management trap we covered in Chapter 9 that we must avoid as coaches: checking the box. What would happen if we didn't check our e-mail first thing in the morning and instead checked in on one of our top performers or team leaders? Face time is field time! Even if you lead a company or division of thousands of people, that's an obstacle that only seems bigger than it really is. Of course, no one can possibly coach thousands of people day to day. But you don't have a team of a thousand people; you have a company of a thousand people. You have a team of vice presidents who report directly to you, each of whom manages a team of directors, each of whom manages a team of supervisors, and on down the line. We can get so wrapped up in the size of the company (in terms of both people and dollars and cents) that we fail to see that the problems big companies have with leadership are often just scaled-up versions of small companies. We exaggerate the size of the company obstacle to make it a better excuse for not coaching.

The solution is not to coach a thousand people but to get out there and coach the people who answer to us directly and, in turn, mandate they do it with their direct reports and pay it forward on down the line. That way, our coaching creates more coaches and more control of what is happening on the field— wherever that field is—whenever there are consequences. For the CEO I worked with, this required visiting plants around the country, and he finally gave in and scheduled "market visits" to his plant managers two times per month. After only ninety days, he told me being out of his office and working with the team made him more aware of what was transpiring in his business than he had been in the past ten years. He now makes it a priority for himself and his direct reports to be in the field with their teams. He went from being a great leader who was successful to a great coach who was making his team better—and making more coaches to coach the teams that reported to them.

My client no longer feels disconnected—unseen, unheard, and at a distance from his team and his company as a whole. He no longer feels so far away, and he not only sees problems before they happen but also what he needs to change from the top. Other leaders may not feel this way and thus not feel the need to get on the field at their organizations. The company may be doing just fine with their managing the way they have been. But I guarantee that if they are not coaching and on the field, they are not being as effective as they could be. They are unaware of problems they would never tolerate though seemingly do because they are not mandating that they or anyone who works for them get on the field to hold anyone accountable.

Of course, leaders cannot know *everything* going on in their businesses, but that can't be an excuse for knowing very little. Coming down from the skybox for the dog and pony show after a big sale, event, or meeting and giving high fives just won't cut it.

In sales, we talk about top-down selling; in coaching, the principles are the same: To ensure a successful coaching culture and reinforce the importance of being in the field, start at the top. Because if I am *not* the CEO and my boss and my boss's boss do not have time to coach me or to go out on the field, then most likely, I will not make the time either, and I won't be motivated to make the time because it has no value. But if, from the top down, they do it, then I bet my week's gas money that I will be out there as well.

We really shouldn't need this top-down approach, since field time is usually the time most leaders say they enjoyed the most before they made it to the C-suite. But because it's the part of the job easiest to eliminate, we need the extra incentive. So why not remember that? Let's spend more time doing the parts of our job we love the most. We'll love our work all the more and we'll get better results.

Coaching Means Never Having to Go Undercover

More than a dozen CEOs at major brands have learned the importance of getting on the field in a very public way on the CBS TV reality show *Undercover Boss*. The show follows chief executives from companies like 7-Eleven, Hooters, and White Castle as they slip anonymously into the rank and file of their companies to see how they are really working. Larry O'Donnell, CEO of Waste Management, was first up. A family man and all-around nice guy, O'Donnell, like many of the CEOs who followed on the show, not only performed the work poorly but also became irritated by some of the rules his managers enforced and by how they enforced them—rules he ostensibly put into place and leaders he indirectly hired in his role as CEO! He was fired from his undercover job.

I am sure Larry O'Donnell and every one of CBS's undercover bosses used at least one of the many excuses for not getting on the field regularly before submitting to the beatdown of the show. Thus, every one of them is surprised by all the good stuff and bad stuff they find going on in the company and realize their detachment was a mistake. Consider that the next time you're inclined to blame someone or something else for a failure in the ranks. These are CEOs of some of the most successful companies in the world! And while I know reality TV like this is not completely "real," consider this as well: It does take time to make the show, and in the weeks it took to set up and shoot *Undercover Boss*, not one CEO complained about the time away from the office—the very excuse so many leaders use for not coaching. Sure, the short-term publicity value was enormous for the companies but my hope is that these CEOs also realize that getting on the field and coaching can have even more enormous long-term benefits.

I know I did when I took over the Southern California market for Sprint. Remember the Snowman and his team from Chapter 4, who resisted my push to set logical, not realistic, goals and become the best market in the country? Turns out, Sprint's problems in California went even deeper than I thought, as I found out when I got on the field with the team and went with the Snowman to one of his stores. The manager of the store told us they knew things had improved with Sprint, but his customers didn't; he knew he could sell more phones and plans if they had the new coverage maps and the right collateral material about Sprint's service. I couldn't figure out why he didn't have them. I knew we had created those maps, so I asked the Snowman where they were. Since his team had no accountability, the Snowman didn't know, so he called the account executive in charge of the store, who told him they had been out of them for months.

I couldn't understand how a multimillion-dollar company in a major market could be out of this essential sales tool, but not wanting to doubt my new team, I called the corporate market manager to complain. He told me, "You're not out of maps. You have twenty-five thousand in cases in your office. Here's where they're located." He was right. I got a giant stack of maps, went to the Snowman's office, tossed them onto his desk, and went back to my office to wait for the Snowman to see them. When he did, he came to my office and said, "Boss, you are a genius, you are awesome. Where did you find these maps?"

"With the other twenty-five thousand in the office," I replied.

Now, I could have been nice to the Snowman and let him

think I was a genius, but that would be validating bad behavior and shying away from conflict. I did not play nice. I confronted him directly to see how he would react. I wasn't going to let him pacify me with compliments or deflect the blame: "I have two questions for you, and only one of these questions applies here: Do I have a manager who is a liar about having the tools to succeed? Or do I have a manager who is incompetent and doesn't know where twenty-five thousand maps are in his office?"

I know that sounds blunt and even aggressive, but the Snowman's behavior and incompetence warranted it. He had already resisted coaching and at every turn had tried to prevent me from holding anyone accountable. By taking that accountability to the field, I turned his world upside down. Under previous management, he was able to cover his you-know-what at every turn with lies and personality, and he created circumstances in which he could look like the best and blame everyone else for his not succeeding more. But, really, he was just lazy and this laziness was exposed when I got on the field with him. Think about it: How often does it happen that after a manager or employee leaves the company, we dig into matters and realize how messed up things were and that the former employee was doing the exact opposite of what we had thought? I know it has happened to me more than once. I had learned to not let it happen with people like the Snowman, who never have the desire to get better and win.

Coaches Need to See the Plays Up Close

When I go in the field with my team, everything I do is to help ensure our success. I make sure they are doing things correctly, recognize a job well done, and help develop their skills and better apply their attributes. I get involved, not to take over, but rather to participate. If we are conducting product trainings for clients, I want to know that we are teaching the way the clients learn and giving the clients value, not wasting their time. I may discuss strategies and scrimmage with a team member prior to meeting with our client. We may scrimmage several times, and if I see an issue, I don't ignore it; I bring it up and address it.

I was very fortunate early in my career to learn from a leader who taught me to make being in the field my number one priority and mandated field time for my managers and myself. My goal was to spend at least three days per week in the field with my managers, sales reps, marketing team members, and clients. Often, I achieved four days per week. My work did not suffer; in fact, it got better. I became better at delegating administrative tasks, not getting too involved in simple issues that others had better abilities and skills to handle, and managing my time so that I could focus on what was most important—developing my team. I allowed myself four hours every day to do my administrative work at the office; I scheduled administrative tasks from seven thirty to nine thirty A.M. and then two hours in the afternoon. The rest of my time was with my team, working with them (not for them).

In life, standing on the sideline often means something negative: inaction on the part of someone who should have taken responsibility. In business and sports, it's the right place to be. Coaches can't and shouldn't play the game or do the work for the team, but they need to be as close as possible to the field to get involved when required and have a true sense of how the team is actually doing. By being present, we are able to observe our talent and make quicker and more accurate decisions to help protect and grow our business. Even if your team is in one office together, this principle can apply if you simply get up from your desk, leave your office, and sit down with the team instead of waiting for them to come to you. Before pressing SEND on an-

other e-mail or text to the team down the hall, get up and imagine the hallway is like the tunnel to their ball field: the
game—meaning anything in business that has consequences—is
out there.

Remember: Be Proud, Not Prideful

In the end, leaders must do every job with the intent of doing our best and not merely getting it done. When we do a job,
no matter what the job is, we want to be proud of our work. But
we also must not let our egos get in the way of our coaching,
especially when we are on the field with the team. We must be
humble in our ability to coach and learn, and confident in our
stature. At the same time, we don't want to be so prideful that
we are threatened every time someone is giving us feedback or
getting involved in our business. This kind of pride causes us to
be defensive and unwilling to listen and grow as leaders. As a
team, our goal is to be the best team, and as their coach, if I am
not being prideful, that team should not be offended or upset
when I am helping us achieve our goals. Remember: Our teams
understand and appreciate a coach's presence. The only time I
would feel threatened by a coach inspecting what I was doing
was if my team and I were not do-
ing our jobs.

**Even Superman can be
pushed to fly higher.**

The best leaders in business,
like the best coaches in sports, did
not get that way because they
think they know all they need to know and have developed their
skills as far as they can be developed. But it can seem that way
when we lose touch. Spending time with our team members,
especially in the service of coaching, is one of the greatest things
we can do for them—and for us! It shows respect. It shows we

204 | NATHAN JAMAIL

care about our teams and appreciate their efforts. It gives us the knowledge we need to lead our teams and help lead our companies. It shows them our desire to win.

Now put down this book and get on the field. Or better yet, take it with you and share it with your team as you start practicing and becoming a coach.

Takeaways:
Get on the Field

- Stop turning obstacles into excuses; get out of your office several times a week.
- Working with and developing your team on the field must become the core of a coach's priorities—anything else is just checking off tasks.
- Size does not matter: Leaders cannot coach one thousand people without turning the leaders who report to them into coaches.
- Don't wait for a TV show to come calling to reconnect and understand how your team performs.
- Being on the field does not take away others' authority; it *gives* them power.

POST-GAME WRAP-UP

My final challenge to us as coaches is this: Try and remember to be grateful no matter the business situation or personal situation. Too often in business, **the power of G.L.A.D. (Gratitude, Love, Attitude, and Desire)** is lost, because it is intangible. "What is the ROI on gratitude and love?" they smirk. "Here we go with that feel-good stuff that doesn't do anything." Many organizations thus tend to skip the meaning of words and focus only on the results of coaching. But these guiding principles should control a coaching culture as much as they should control all things in life. They determine our success and sustainability as much as any result that can be measured on a spreadsheet.

Being **GRATEFUL** means appreciating that everything we have is a blessing. When we are grateful for what we have, we are not envious of what others have

> It is our gratitude that will give us great fortitude.

and we are not jealous of their success; instead we are intrigued by how we may be able to achieve similar success. Coaches should admire rather than resent the successes of others. They need to focus on obtaining more success for their team without ever losing sight that making a team better cannot be at the expense of being better people.

We can't be fully successful as coaches or teammates if we don't **LOVE** our jobs. Love motivates us to keep going in spite of the bad days. When we love our jobs, we are happier and, consequently, everyone around us is happier. That's why I insist that everybody on my team love his or her job. This has caused some controversy over the years with my bosses, employees, and sometimes with HR. Despite this controversy, my insistence has, in the long run, always proven to be true and effective. To leaders who tell me it is an unrealistic expectation to have a team on which everybody loves their job, I say to them, "You might be right." Their belief might make it true for them. Not me. My bottom line is this: If we are unhappy, stressed and/or anxious as coaches, our teams can *feel* it.

Teams can also feel a bad **ATTITUDE**, which is overall a bigger determiner of success than education, money, parents, or family tree. I understand that not every minute of every day is positive, but how we spend the rest of those days is our choice. This means much more than trying to be happy or smiling. Dream and think big as a coach and you will become BIG—especially in the eyes of your team. When someone tells you that you can't do it, laugh it off and use it as fuel as you fly toward your goals. I believe someone has to be number one, so why not me? Or if someone can do it, then so can I. Some may call this naïve or even ignorant, yet I still believe it to be true (and it has proven itself over and over again in my world and for those I coach).

After all, many teams have won games by luck or chance and have lost games in which they did everything right, but having the **DESIRE** to fight every day to achieve our goals means we will be winners even when we lose. Desire is what we need to take action to support that attitude. It is the drive to do what it takes to achieve your goals. Desire gives a salesperson the ability to call another prospect after getting rejected, an operations manager the ability to keep focusing on the solution when her department faces adversity, or a designer the ability to remake a project when the first model gets destroyed. As a coach or a leader in business, we must be able to help our team find this desire. Otherwise they will become discouraged when faced with adversity, or complacent in times of comfort.

Simply put, G.L.A.D. makes us great, and if we ignore it, our teams will start to ignore it too and we are left with actions without emotional attachment. Imagine life without an emotional connection and drive—it becomes fruitless and empty. We know the importance of these guiding principles, but they get lost in the craziness of trying to maintain them.

To keep my focus, I carry my "Power and Prosperity" coin wherever I go. You can use a coin, a rock, a button, a picture, or a leaf for all it matters. The point is to have a tool to help you focus on what matters as a coach. My coin helps me to focus on G.L.A.D. every day. Being **Grateful** for what I have and who I am, **Loving** myself and what I do, having the **Attitude** to know and believe that I can be number one, and fueling the **Desire** to do what it takes to achieve it.

ACKNOWLEDGMENTS

I can't believe that I have been blessed with this great opportunity to share my thoughts and experiences with so many people. It has been humbling and rewarding and never would have been possible without the many blessings I have been given and the love and support of my family.

My wife, Shannon, who is the greatest human being I have ever met, has not only given me four beautiful kids—Anthony, Nyla, Paige, and Savannah—but is the person who makes all of this possible. I could fill ten pages with how great she is, but she would just tell me to "shut up and move on." I love you, baby, now and forever.

And my parents, who have been the most influential people in my life and, no matter what, loved me and supported me, even when we all knew I didn't deserve it. I can only pray that I have been and will be as good a parent to my kids as they were to my brothers and me.

Thank you, Joe Calloway, for still accepting my calls after eight years and always being willing to help and guide me down the right path. I also want to thank my many clients who have allowed me to work with them and have taught me so much more than I could ever teach them.

Thanks to all of my past leaders, team members, and business partners, because without your guidance, knowledge, and advice, I would not have had any ideas or experiences to share.

To Wendy Keller: I am so grateful. Without your reaching out to me, asking me to write another leadership book, and your advice and partnership, this book would not have even started—not to mention my immense gratitude for introducing me to Jim Eber.

Jim was the one who put it all together. Many days and nights were spent Skyping with Jim to assemble this book (or, more specifically, he took my jumble and made it make sense). You are the man!

Lastly, thanks to the team that makes sure everything is done right and at the highest quality: the Penguin Random House publishing company. To Lauren Marino for all of her insight and tough love to make sure the book is the best it can be, and to the rest of the all-star Penguin team: Farin Schlussel, Anne Kosmoski, Lisa Johnson, and every one of the hardworking individuals behind the scenes. It is an absolute honor to work with the best in the business.